YORKSHIRE GYPSY FAIRS CUSTOMS AND CARAVANS 1885-1985

by

E. ALAN JONES

With a Foreword by
FIONA SCOTT

HUTTON PRESS

1986

Published by the Hutton Press Ltd.
130 Canada Drive, Cherry Burton, Beverley
East Yorkshire HU17 7SB

First published 1986
Reprinted with corrections, 1987
Reprinted 1989
Reprinted 1991
Reprinted 1993

Printed by Clifford Ward & Co.
(Bridlington) Ltd.
55 West Street, Bridlington, East Yorkshire
YO15 3DZ

ISBN 0 907033 43 1

To Pat, Sarah and Kathrine
for allowing me to follow
my other great love.

FOREWORD

The first commission I received when I opened my studio at Helmsley early this year, was from Alan Jones for a painting of his attractive Georgian Workshop at Malton. Inside the workshop and outside on the signboards are images of Gypsy caravans. These are the trademarks of Alan Jones's craft and until I read this book I had no idea of the skill and dedication needed in the decoration and restoration of gypsy caravans.

Not only is Mr. Jones an expert in this work, but he also has a wide knowledge and understanding of the Travelling people. The gypsies, their history, customs, caravans and present way of life are clearly described and I know that Alan Jones's book will surely stimulate your interest.

Fiona Scott
Helmsley, North Yorkshire
1st June 1987

4

CONTENTS

ACKNOWLEDGEMENTS

The Author wishes to thank the following for providing material for this book:
Abbey Galleries (Whitby) Ltd.; Ackrill Newspapers Ltd.; A.R.B. (Oxo).
BBC Radio York; Mr. Denzil Bone; Mr. Tony Boxall; the "Brighouse Echo,"
in particular Mr. Ralph Wade; Mr. Charles Brook of the Hutton Press; the
Brotherton Library, the University of Leeds.
The Castle Museum, York, in particular Mr. Mark Suggett; Mr. Andrew
Church; Cobdale Trailers Ltd.; Cottage Books; "Country Life"; the "Craven
Herald" Ltd.; Cusworth Hall Museum, Doncaster.
Mr. J. W. Dawson.
Rev. Malcolm Exley, Market Weighton.
The Farrow family; Mr. Ron Finch;
Richard Gill & Sons Ltd.; Mr. John Goodchild; the "Goole Times."
The Hartlepool "Mail"; Mr. Dave Hartley; Denis Harvey:"The Gypsies;
Waggon-time and After." Batsford, 1979, reprinted 1984; C.H. Ward-Jackson
and Denis Harvey: "The English Gypsy Caravan." David & Charles, 1972.
New ed. 1986; the Home Office; Mr. Michael Horsley; the "Hull Daily Mail," in
particular Miss Janice Hunter; the Hull Heritage Centre, in particular Ms.
Belinda Moores; Mr. and Mrs. P. M. Hyam.
Mr. and Mrs. Johnson and the Hill family from Swinefleet, Goole; Mr. Mervyn
Jones.
Leeds Tourist Information Centre; Mrs. Sue Lilley; the University of Liverpool.
The Malton area travellers; the Malton Bookshop; Mrs. Dorothy Morrison.
Northern Counties Newspapers (Yorkshire) Ltd.; the "Northern Echo," in
particular Mr. Peter Chapman and Mr. Paul Hines.
Paultons Park & Bird Gardens, Ower, Romsey, Hants.
Mr. Richard Robson, Curator, Castle Howard Costume Gallery; the Royal
Crown Derby Porcelain Co. Ltd; Mr. Brian Raywid: "Reminiscences of Life on
the Roads." In Journal of the Gypsy Lore Society. Vol. LI, Pts 3 & 4, 1972.
Save the Children Fund U.K.; Mr. Basil Smith; Mr. D. Smith, Curator, Ryedale
Folk Museum; Peter Smith Photography, Malton; Smith & Wellstood Ltd.;
Stockton on Tees Borough Council Museum Service; Strickland & Holt Ltd.,
Yarm and York. Michael Scales Photography, Malton.
Mr. John Thompson; Topcliffe Parish Council.
Mr. M. G. J. Vasey.
Mr. D. A. Waddingham; Wakefield Metropolitan District Council; Rev. Jack
Walker, North Newbald; the "Whitby Gazette"; Whiteheads of Appleby; the
Wood family; the World's Fair, Oldham.
Yorkshire Weekly Newspaper Group Ltd.

INTRODUCTION

At the end of the eighteenth century scholars were able to determine the origin of the Gypsies on the basis of scientific evidence. This was done by making a study of the language and the areas that it originated from. It was found that their speech was very similar to the Sanskrit and Hindi variations of the local dialect from Northern India. During this period it is recorded that 12,000 musicians of the Zott (or Gypsy) tribe had arrived in Persia from India and, whilst this large number all in the same profession is most unlikely, there were certainly many Gypsies in Persia at this time.

From Persia it is believed that the Gypsies split into two tribes. One went West and South East and the other went North West via Armenia ending their journey in Europe. In 1418, after being in Greece and Turkey, groups went through Hungary and Germany where they were given letters of protection. However, these letters were not valid in France where they first appeared in 1419. In 1427 they arrived at the gates of Paris for the first time when this city was occupied by the English. They camped for three weeks and were visited by curious locals who had never seen their like before.

In the sixteenth century the Gypsies arrived in Scotland and England for the first time. It is not known if they came direct from France, but for the next two hundred years all the European countries had their Gypsies. Countries such as Spain and Portugal actually deported them at this time to places like Angola and Brazil. In the seventeenth century Gypsies from Scotland were sent to Jamaica and Barbados to work in the plantations. It must be presumed that they were wrongdoers in some way to warrant this kind of treatment. They were also sent to Virginia, other parts of America, Argentina and Chile.

For the last 1,000 years the Gypsies have been on the move from Northern India through Europe. The largest number of travellers settled in Eastern Europe but others went into Spain and the South of France and eventually to the British Isles in the North.

When they travelled round the countryside either on the Continent or in this country Gypsies were in large bands or groups and tended to intimidate the local population by virtue of their unkempt appearance. It is reported that Scotland had its first recorded Gypsy in 1504 (or Little Egyptian as they were known because it was thought that they had come from Egypt). As most of the records were completed by clerks of the local magistrates all the people mentioned in their books were the lawbreakers of the time. The normal everyday traveller, minding his or her business, went by without a mention.

From Scotland it was only a short haul down into Yorkshire. By the middle of the last century the West Riding of Yorkshire was a busy, and thriving, industrial area. The mills were all in full employment and the demand for horses to pull delivery vehicles was great. Who better to supply these needs than the Gypsy people? Working both from the countryside, where fodder and free grazing could be obtained, and from the cities where there was a demand for labour, the traveller could manage a living. Being generally a handy person he used to offer his services for repairing machinery and metal objects like pots and pans. The MacFie sugar refinery at Rawcliffe in the West Riding, before

1893 known as Duncans refinery, used travellers to mend the large copper vats both in Yorkshire and in their main works at Liverpool.

The population census of the mid 1960's stated that there were 692 (nomadic) Gypsies in the area of the West Riding of Yorkshire. This would only be about one fifth of the Yorkshire total with large gatherings at Middlesbrough, Doncaster, Hull, and smaller groups scattered in the towns and villages. Since 1978 counts of Gypsy caravans, Gypsies and their families have been carried out twice a year by the District Authorities in England for the Department of the Environment. The first national count was in 1965 by the Old Ministry of Housing and Local Government and was followed by many partial surveys by the Gypsy organisations themselves in the 1970's.

In 1976 the Department of the Environment analysed all the figures available and came to the conclusion that there were in the region of 9,000 families in England and Wales. Based on this information Sir John Cripps published in 1977 his report called 'Accommodation for Gypsies' which concluded that there must be about 40,000 Gypsies all told. Due to the haphazard way these figures had been obtained, the Government in its wisdom decided to do a count twice a year on the same dates to avoid duplication and the first of these was on the 12th of July 1978. In January and July on the Wednesday nearest to the 15th of the month a form is sent out to all District Councils and their returns indicidate the number of caravans, Gypsies and families, and types of site. These have been regularly filled in and returned so that a fair count could be done, with very few authorities not bothering to do so. For instance in January 1982 only seven districts out of 366 did not return their completed forms. Whilst some areas do not always manage to obtain the information required from caravans parked without permission, the counts on the official sites are accurate.

What is shown from all this paperwork is that in 1979 there were 8,400 Gypsy caravans (not the horse-drawn type!) in England and in 1982 there were 8,800, so the numbrs have remained fairly static over a four-year period. Figures themselves prove nothing and can be manipulated to suit the needs of those that compile them but in England over a three-year period from 1979 to 1981 the Gypsy population averaged around the twenty-seven thousand mark, including adults and children. The numbers of caravans in 1982 in Yorkshire and Humberside show that there were 490 on authorised encampments, 220 on council authorised sites and 55 on private authorised sites making a total of 765 in all.

No figures are available for the days of the horse-drawn caravan but one can only guess that the numbers have increased over the years as people have transferred to modern vehicles and have also been joined by house-dwellers who may have defaulted on rents and opted for what they think is an alternative life style.

Returning to the days of the horse-drawn caravans, in places like the West Riding of Yorkshire the traveller being adaptable would eventually set himself up with a horse-drawn vehicle and make use of roller fabric covers from the mills for insulation over the bow-top roof under the waterproof canvas. Some of the mill workers also fancied this apparent freedom and purchased a horse and made a rough sort of accommodation for themselves. They would go out for short periods into the countryside around the industrial cities. Eventually they got to like this way of life and their descendants are still about today dealing in scrap metal and other lines like rolls of carpeting, or working in tarmac or in the building trade.

Over the years the Gypsy people have been regarded with suspicion, maybe because they have tended to be very much a people who keep themselves to themselves, never liking to interfere in the lives of those they occasionally find round them, and always thought to be on the scrounge or even tempted sometimes to be dishonest to obtain what they required. This may, or may not, be so. However is not the office worker also slightly dishonest at times? Does he not take time off for a smoke in working hours and take home pens and pencils from his workplace because they are of such small value in themselves? Add up his time, which he is being paid for, and his lifted items over a twelve-month period and he might be classed as expensively dishonest!

Throughout Europe the Gypsy was always moved on, in case he did any misdemeanour and over the years he has never had a settled home; always blamed for any misdeeds in the area even if he did not commit them, blamed if livestock went missing and often accused of stealing children. The last was something he would never do as he always had plenty of his own!

Townfolk would ban Gypsies and flog and beat them if they arrived, constantly trying to discourage the traveller from settling and keeping him on the move. Sometimes Gypsies were beaten up by the local population for nothing more than just being in their town or village. In other cases the locals would take the law into their own hands and actually execute individuals as a warning to others. This happened in York in 1596 when the magistrates made Gypsy children watch while their parents were executed. Presumably this was done on the Knavesmire at the same place where Dick Turpin was hanged as he too was regarded with awe and considered to operate outside the law. The Gypsies in York, however, were hanged as an example to others just because they were who they were.

The English Gypsy never was a highwayman in the real sense. He did not specialise in this form of robbery as he did with horse stealing, but even so there are a few recorded cases. Because of their continual travelling on the highways and byeways they must have been open to temptation on occasions. The City of York records in 1650 mention certain Greys and Parkers as highway robbers, though this is well before the period we are interested in. The practice of stripping and robbing people was common from the 1660's to the early 1700's. Clothing itself was a very saleable item but up to the middle of the 1800's the risk was great as people were still being transported for their crimes. Court cases of the time refer to people being 'juggled' out of their money and this could mean that they and their money were parted by the good old Gypsy fortune teller.

For the last few centuries the persecution of the Romany people has continued by groups of so-called civilised folk. Even today in towns, cities, and to some extent, the countryside the descendants of the original Gypsy settlers are hounded and moved on. The law is slightly kinder now than it used to be, but even so Gypsy people cannot stop where they wish. Instead they are expected to conform and maybe settle down on a permanent site provided by the local authority.

The Caravan Sites Act of 1968 gave the local authorities the statutory duty to provide sites for Gypsies. Prior to this date the Caravan Sites and Control of Development Act 1960 gave the authority the power to provide sites if they wished but they did not have to do so. From the travellers' point of view the 1968 Act meant that the police were not able to keep moving them on if the authority had no spare places unless they were parked on council-owned land for more than twenty-eight days.

Once a council had provided a site for about 15 to 20 units then it could apply to the Department of the Environment for a Designation Order. If the Department agreed that this Order should be made, then a Statutory Instrument must be laid before Parliament for forty days. If no objections to this have been made by a Member of Parliament or a Member of the House of Lords, approval is given without debate.

Whilst these Acts and the implementation of the designated areas are not, in my view, a substitute for freedom of choice they do seem to offer some sort of legal protection. In the past when travellers were on the roads in horse-drawn vehicles the law would always keep them on the move unless they had illness in the family or a lame horse or something of that nature whereby they could not move. Today, whilst in modern mobile homes, a procedure has to be followed. In a designated area the Gypsies can be moved without the land-owner's permission but only after a police summons which requires the local authority to apply to the magistates' court. All this takes time and the traveller in the meantime cannot be hassled by the law whilst this procedure is being carried out.

So, from their journey across Europe during the last 600 years the Gypsy has dispersed throughout our country making his living by filling a need: scrap metal collecting, basket and pot mending, supplying any items and services needed by the area in which he travelled. Sadly since the Second World War and the spread of industrialisation the travellers have had to take on factory or agricultural work even though in the main they prefer to be their own boss and independent.

The intention of this book is not be to a complete history of the Romany people, as this has been done more fully elsewhere, but to show the non-Gypsy a little of the way of life, the nature of the people and maybe to explain why they act and think in a different way to the house-dweller. With this understanding there should be no reason why the two societies may not exist in perfect harmony.

This is my wish.

E.A.J.
Malton, North Yorkshire.
September 1986

CHAPTER ONE

WAY OF LIFE, CUSTOMS, HABITS, DRESS AND EARNINGS

Gypsies practice various trades: tin smithing, basket making, collectors of scrap metal, entertaining as musicians, and so on. Whilst travelling they also time their journeys to be near fruit or hop-picking in the South or general farm work like sugar beet harvesting, potato picking, land draining, ditching and corn harvesting here in the North of England at the appropriate point in the season.

Generally they love to buy and sell. Hawking and dealing is a favourite money-making venture for them. You would never, or very very rarely, find a Gypsy employed on a permanent basis. He is usually offered part-time work with his skill and labour provided strictly on a cash basis.

From the turn of this century to about the 1950's the horse-drawn caravan was the most common form of dwelling used by the travellers. Work could be picked up on a casual basis in most areas of Yorkshire: scrap in the cities and

Mr. C.M. Womersley pulling away from Holme-on-Spalding Moor, East Yorkshire, en route for his home at Chapletown, Sheffield, after three weeks on the road. Note the rich paintwork with superb scrolls on the outside.

11

farmwork in the country. The Gypsy always likes to remain a Gypsy even in a non-Gypsy community. This can sometimes be to his disadvantage and can isolate him and his needs. His way of earning a living being different from the 'nine to five' brigade, he is regarded with suspicion by the non-Gypsy population.

In the present day it is harder for the Gypsy to be able to make a living by offering the kind of services he used to. Mending pots and pans or repairing chairs with cane has very little call today. Due to the development of transport this century, the traditional Gypsy trades can be provided from the towns and cities a lot quicker and cheaper.

Living in horse-drawn waggons in the lanes seems to the non-Gypsy a very ideal and romantic way to spend one's days. Consider the daily routine. Winter would be harder than summer. Imagine waking up in the waggon on a cold, snowy, frosty morning, your breath turning to ice and everything you touch below freezing point; climbing out of the warm bunk at the rear of the vehicle and putting on frozen boots; having dressed and looked out of the waggon to a scene of snow and ice and dying for a warm cup of tea to start the day only to find that the water is also frozen solid. First a fire must be lit and the water boiled. Once a fire is well established, either the outside one, or the small internal 'Queenie' stove, life takes on a new more pleasant slant. Waking up on a beautiful sunny spring or summer day would be idyllic and it is this picture of the travelling way of life that seems firmly embedded in the non-Gypsy mind. In today's modern trailer the pattern is not so bad but whilst the inside may be cosier the outside world is still as cold and frosty in winter. Always assuming that a good park has been found near to a water supply and maybe a shop for everyday needs like tea, hardly ever coffee, sugar and milk, then life is reasonably comfortable.

The menfolk would busy themselves with the daily routine chores of collecting and sorting scrap, repairing and maintaining vehicles and, in the case of the horse-drawn unit, keeping the horse's leather harness clean and polished and in good state of repair. Gathering wood for the fire and locating water are all jobs that form a very time-consuming but very important part of the day's routine. Time itself has no meaning for the traveller. He does not work from nine to five but completes jobs as they need doing or as they present themselves to him. Money is made when required or as the opportunity arrives and if visitors call then a cup of tea is always brewed and time is found to sit and talk and to renew old friendships, something that the non-Gypsy people are more inclined to consider a waste of time and not productive enough. It is usually left to the women to run the home and family.

From childhood, families know each other well as they may travel the same areas and attend the same fairs. It is therefore not unusual for the children to grow up knowing each other and in due course maybe to marry.

Yorkshire Gypsies, in common with all Gypsies, have a high regard for pre-nuptial chastity, and occasionally elopement follows a brief, sometimes very brief, courtship.

The fairs and horse sales have been the annual meeting places where families would always see each other and exchange news and gossip. The young ones

(Above) Family group near Bishop Burton, East Yorkshire, in the 1960's, showing the more popular 'Open-lot' waggon favoured in the Yorkshire area.

(Left) Mr. Peter Farrow in Laundry Lane, Swinton, near Malton, North Yorkshire, with Open-lot style of caravan.

(Below) Open-lot with covers and pneumatic tyres on the Whitwell-on-the-Hill to Foston road in 1985.

might even get the chance to talk and become better acquainted at these events. Eventually they might make a decision to run away together. There would be a show of anger and threats of beatings if they were found by the older members of the two families. However after a few days, or even weeks, the happy couple usually would return and all would be forgiven.

As recently as 1984 I was asked by a young traveller to meet him in Malton Market Place in half an hour's time. When I asked him if the business could not be conducted there and then I was informed that it must be done at 11 o'clock prompt. Explaining that I could not return at that precise time I thought nothing more about it until a few days later when I learned that the young man had arranged to be married at Malton Registry Office in the Market Place at 11 a.m. and needed a witness. Only his intended bride knew about this and there was trouble for months from both families, but happily things have now sorted themselves out and all is well. Tradition continues!

Having previously mentioned the Gypsies' chastity, this was not always practised, as a few well-known families lived with other partners for various lengths of time before actually settling down for life.

If couples decided to part it was a very informal affair, as indeed had been the original elopement, and they were then free to remarry if they so wished. Prior to an elopement topmost security was observed but occasionally the couple would inform their elders with little hints. For instance whilst all were sitting round the fire a young girl may pass her drinking cup to her intended young man and he would also drink from it. If they were not actually betrothed this was considered a very forward practice on behalf of the young woman who would be reprimanded by her elders in no uncertain terms.

The simplest form of marriage vow is the joining of hands in front of witnesses. Early in the 1900's some cases of marriage were described thus. The bride and bridegroom mixed a few drops of their blood with flour which was baked into a small loaf and then shared between them and eaten. Sometimes the blood was not mixed and baked but allowed to flow into a small cup and simply drunk by each party to bind the transaction.

This blood mixing custom may have had its origin in India where a more elaborate form is found in certain tribes. The English Gypsy may be subconsciously continuing an age-old custom from his ancestors in India. It is interesting to note that one hundred years ago the Scottish Gypsies had another wedding custom. A large wooden bowl that held about eight pints was given to the bride at the wedding ceremony for her to urinate into and then to the bridegroom for the same purpose. The official at the wedding would add soil from the ground where they were and sometimes a quantity of whisky and stir the contents together. He would then pass the bowl to the couple in turn and ask them to separate the contents. As they obviously could not, it was presumed that the couple were then married and their union would also be inseparable.

The thought goes through my mind at this point that the ceremony could be the origin of the modern custom of wedding cake. All the various ingredients mixed together with no chance of separating them and small portions given to guests as a symbol of total union. I wonder?

In the North of England after the wedding, shortbread was crumbled over the heads of both bride and bridegroom. East Yorkshire favoured cake instead of shortbread but with a difference — they threw the cake and the plate it was on! Other areas used oatcake, corn, oatmeal, cheese or wheat to wish the pair 'Good Luck.' Today we use confetti.

Many of you will have heard of the tradition of jumping over the brush for a wedding ceremony. The bride and bridegroom would jump over a branch of flowering broom (for fertility). A small posy or ring of flowers would be placed over the bride's wedding finger to be replaced as soon as possible with a gold ring: the ring to be purchased with money earned by both parties so that its cost was shared and therefore a shared partnership for life.

There are many reports on and variations of the wedding ceremony but it must be borne in mind that these basically are hearsay and will have been altered with the telling.

In the 1920's a certain Riley Boswell is reputed to have jumped the broomstick near Driffield in East Yorkshire. This was not taken too seriously as sometimes a mock ceremony would take place every time Gypsies stopped. Music was provided and the locals were charged a fee to witness what they presumed to be an authentic Romany wedding. All monies collected were 'to help the bride and bridegroom.' Quite a profitable venture!

Following the wedding, in due course, a birth would be imminent. The womenfolk followed very strict rules prior to, during, and after the birth. Many of these customs appear to originate in India and have travelled with the people to our shores.

Never would a woman let her hair down in a public place, especially when men were present, as this practice was done by women just prior to childbirth and it was considered by them to give an easier labour. Due to the man's belief that a woman was most unclean at this time he associated the letting down of hair with it and would always walk away.

In the days of the horse-drawn caravan provision would be made for the expectant mother by placing new clean straw on the ground under the waggon or in a nearby canvas tent erected specially for the purpose. Hence the term 'born on the straw,' which a true Romany is very proud to have been born on.

New-born infants in some countries are washed in warm water, but in Yorkshire, along with the Welsh, Manx and German Gypsies, cold running water is used from a nearby stream. As soon as is practically possible the new baby is baptised. Whilst the Gypsy is not a great Churchgoer he does respect the Church and in his own way is God fearing. Living close to nature in all its forms he sees first hand the ways of God and respects them. Taking the religious beliefs of the country and surroundings he finds himself in he very soon adapts to the local ways. Many Churches in Yorkshire are popular with the travelling people but one especially is worth a mention here: the Parish Church of St. Nicholas, North Newbald, East Yorkshire. This Norman Church in a most historic village is situated on the edge of the Plain of York on rising land en route for Hull and the River Humber. It has a beautiful carved door surround depicting the Dog of Heaven held back by Nature, carved into the pillar support and the original old wood door is complete with hundreds of old iron nails used in the past for fixing village notices and news sheets. The Church was built with local labour used for all the main walls and stonework; the arches and carvings were completed by French masons. It was built and used by people many years before the great York Minster and it is to this Church that many of the East Riding Gypsies go for their family events. It is traditional here for babies to be baptised within three Sundays of birth whilst it is general practice for people to be buried in the Parish that they die, wherever that may be.

If a husband has left the family because of an argument or difference of opinion or for any other reason, and the wife thinks he may stay away, an old custom was to pass a baby through a split ash tree sapling or branch and this would hopefully bring him back.

From birth Gypsy children are always loved and cared for. A non-Gypsy would almost say that they were spoilt as most of their demands are met where possible. Sweets are a great favourite with the youngsters and one must always remember to be armed with pockets full of assorted kinds when visiting travelling friends with young children!

The child is brought up in the family unit, helping with chores from an early age and learning the ways of the travelling life from its parents. Boys will start helping their fathers with the horses, attending fairs and listening to deals being made, from a very young age. Whilst not actively taking part they are subconsciously learning for their own future survival. Girls are instructed by their mothers in the general domestic jobs like cooking ,washing and bringing up a family, as most times there will be other brothers and sisters of various ages and all will have to help each other.

For many years the Gypsy people have dressed in their own special way. The women would wear long skirts reaching to the ankles, fitting tightly at the waist and with a round yolk of white lace at the neck, normally in plain unpatterned colours of dark blue, amber, cherry red or crimson and worn with a wide-brimmed, beaver-trimmed, black straw hat with ostrich feathers. Gypsy women have always favoured the high-legged, high-heeled brown or black laced 'Luton' boots that could be seen peeping out from under copious white embroidered underskirts. Young girls would be dressed in grey, blue or red-printed cotton gingham still full length and cut in the 'wasp-waisted' Gypsy fashion. Sometimes a pocket was sewn into an underskirt or maybe a separate little bag was worn on a belt round the waist to hold money or valuables gathered whilst out calling.

The menfolk tended to wear brown or green suits made from thick material, with five or six pockets, one of which on the inside would be large enough to pop a hare or rabbit into if the need arose. If not a matching suit then the jacket was worn with moleskin trousers with a drop-fronted fly with heavy stitching like the jacket. A trilby or flat cap was worn on the head with a bright-coloured silk scarf knotted round the neck to complete the outfit. Modern young travellers like the wide pin-stripe suit in grey, blue or brown or worn with a wide leather belt and red clip-on braces, all set off with a pair of brown elastic-sided dealer boots.

In the spring, Romany children would make baskets out of hazel twigs packed with moss and filled with posies of wild flowers, which would be sold either door to door or at fairs in the area. Spring is an interesting time in the travellers' life as there are plenty of fresh herbs and vegetables, horses giving birth to their foals, and generally all things in abundance.

Herbs from the hedgerows and fields form a very important part of the travellers' diet and the womenfolk were always very knowledgeable about their use. In days gone by, and somewhat less so today, they tended to keep this knowledge secret as they wished to have the 'know how' to heal and to be able to charge for it. Healing with herbs has always been practiced by the Gypsies even though they do attend the doctor's surgery when the need arises for their more serious complaints.

We have always lived in a stress-related world though today seems to be more so. Families have always had the worry of survival and the need to be able to provide food and clothing so it is really a matter of degree which is the more stress-laden age.

Taking drugs continually will confuse the body-chemicals and the balance of nature is altered and might prove a problem. When drugs are stopped the body is so confused that it still cannot get back to its original pattern so the patient assumes, wrongly, that he needs the drugs and starts to take them again. If he left the body well alone it might right itself after a few days into a normal pattern. If, however, the problem does continue for any length of time then a doctor should be consulted as many things could be causing it.

For a good night's sleep instead of tea or coffee one should have milky drinks or herb teas last thing at night. The Romany would use herbs like chamomile, lemon balm, or hops, the last being either in his beer or as a dried herb in his pillow! Cowslips, lavender, fennel and peppermint all make excellent teas. Not all these herbs are readily available from nature due either to location or time of the year but they can nearly always be purchased from health food shops or chemists. However, a very simple herb that most people overlook, or do not even think of as a herb, is lettuce. This can be grown almost anywhere and may be eaten raw or made into a soup with milk and grated nutmeg, providing a suitable nightcap for the non-sleeper.

Medicines in Britain were formerly herbal and all modern drugs stem from these. Many today take only one or two ingredients from a plant and this may cause side effects as the whole plant is needed for the cure. In the country the traveller could never extract the ingredients from the plant and would automatically use all of it for his cure. In days gone by the whole herb was used either raw as a wrap round a sore or cut, or boiled as a poultice and therefore all the active particles would be in contact with the patient providing a total balance. It is only in the last one hundred years that medicines have taken any really great steps forward. The Romans and other invaders to our shores are mainly responsible for introducing our herb cures. Fresh herbs when available are good but, amazing as it may seem, the dried herb is about three or four times stronger so less is actually used.

A scientist called Dr. Charles J. McAlister in the 1930's realised the healing powers of the comfrey plan must contain some extra special property. By experimentation he managed to isolate the chemical allantoin and for the first time there was a scientific reason for the plant's magical powers. Known to the Romany as 'Knitbone' the comfrey plant's botanical name is "Symphytum Officinale," which comes from the Greek and means union or joining together. It is excellent in the treatment of bruises and rashes, burns, scalds or sprains. Many claims are made over its use to fight cancer, ulcers and other ailments but these may, or may not, be correct. As well as allantoin comfrey contains vitamin B12 and gives a very much needed boost to some diets lacking this essential vitamin. It is best eaten in spring, when the new leaf is tender, either in sandwiches or in salads. Boiled and drunk as a tea with lemon or honey added it is also very refreshing. Dried leaves in the autumn stored away to be used in the winter months are a must. The plant dies down at the first sign of frost and so the fresh leaves are not available in the winter. The discovery of allantoin showed that the plant contained the ingredient which caused skin cells to proliferate and to promote the growth of new tissue. This explains why it was so popular in folk medicine as an ointment and poultice.

Many wild plants are used as medicines, tonics, and cures for both horse and human. The common nettle, found almost everywhere, when boiled and eaten with a knob of butter resembles spinach. Soup made from young tender nettles is superb and rich in vitamins and iron. It is supposedly good for rheumatism sufferers.

The fast-growing herb feverfew, often found on waste land, with its white daisy-like flower and chrysanthemum leaves, is a member of the chrysanthemum family and originally came from China. When eaten fresh the leaf has a very bitter taste but can be disguised in a sandwich or salad or made into a tea where it is a real boon to the migraine sufferer.

Dandelions can be eaten when young in salad or drunk as a tea but even better still made into a wine using the yellow flower heads when in season. If the roots are dug up and washed, then roasted and ground they make an excellent coffee substitute. It is not a real coffee taste and can in fact be mixed with the instant brands to make them go further and taste more like actual coffee. Drunk instead of coffee it is a great tonic and 'pick you up' for many minor internal disorders. The juice extract is good for the liver and for gall bladder disorders and gall stones as well as helping the bladder by eliminating excess water and poisons in both the kidneys and the liver. It also lowers the level of acids that cause rheumatism.

The raspberry leaf is used by women travellers in a tea form. Taken a few weeks before giving birth as a teacup full a day it is said to reduce bleeding. Yarrow is also an aid to childbirth drunk as a tea by helping to bring away the afterbirth easier because it has the effect of tightening the uterus. Dill seeds made into a tea by adding half a cup of boiling water to one teaspoonful of seeds, strained and cooled then given to baby as a gripe water helps with its digestion.

Many wild herbs grow in great abundance on the roadsides but one should not collect them if traffic fumes, dirt and grime have tainted them. One should try to obtain herbs from a clean natural place where one will get the full benefit from the plant itself.

As well as herbs, wild honey is very important to the general health and well being of the travelling people. If they were lucky they would be able to locate the combs of wild honey in the countryside. Today bees are kept and worked artificially and their hives located in positions which suit the keeper. In nature the bee would select the best pollens of the area to produce truly top quality honey. From this hard worker we obtain the minerals iron, manganese, copper, calcium, potassium, sodium, phosphorus, silica and others to a lesser degree. The plant takes these into its system and the bee in turn takes them from the nectar. Vitamins, especially vitamin C, are contained in honey and are most important for our good health. Used as a sedative, one spoonful two or three times a day will help induce sleep at night and enable the individual to abandon sleeping tablets. Honey has been well known as a cough remedy and with lemon added is a favourite with young and old alike. Said to be an aphrodisiac this golden wonder is also a natural laxative and helps keep a good clean complexion. Placed on burns it relieves the pain and prevents blisters from forming. A hayfever allergy is said to be helped by taking a spoonful every day of the honey made by bees that have collected pollen from the area that causes the suffering. However, any honey could relieve the symptoms if taken daily.

Understanding nature comes easily to the true countryman and he uses its free bounty to the full: not only animals to cook and eat with the wild herbs but also fruit, nuts and berries in their seasons. The main berry or fruit picked and enjoyed by the traveller and the town dweller alike is the blackberry. This is a pleasure in the early autumn and provides a final chance to partake of nature's harvest before the harshness of winter sets in. Very full of vitamin C when eaten raw, in a pie, or as a cordial it gives the badly needed boost against colds and 'flu during the colder days to follow. The hips from the dog rose if collected and made into a syrup are also a vital source of vitamin C. Many will remember collecting hips during and just after the Second World War to be processed into syrup for babies to make them grow up big and healthy. Elderberries, after the beautiful winemaking scented flowers, fill the hedgerows in autumn and make a superb wine themselves or a cordial if preferred. If a few cloves are added in preparation they enhance the flavour and can be used with hot water as a pre-bedtime drink or to relieve the discomfort of cold and chestiness.

Hazel nuts provide a good supply of protein and like all nuts prefer a hot summer and a dry autumn to produce the best quality and quantity.

Over the years the Romany has always used nature's larder for the good of his health, a fact now being put into practice by the non-Gypsy via the large commercial influences.

Whilst on the subject of herbs and good things to eat found in nature it may be worth mentioning at this point a little about Romany cooking. The family life of the travelling people centres round the camp fire and the cooking pot. The fire provides the heat and warmth both for the people and the contents of the cooking pot. When a fire is first made on a new site a large turf should be removed and placed away from the heat to be replaced later. Large sticks about two or three inches in diameter are positioned like the spokes of a wheel from the centre of where the fire will be. On top of this the smaller pieces of twig, leaves and dried bark are added with a final topping off of large dry logs. The air travels up the space between the spoke-shaped base and gives the fire

A most impressive Bow-top caravan in a North Yorkshire lane clearly showing the spreader (holding lamp) for fixing an additional horse for uphill pulling.

20

(Above) Roadside scene between York and Easingwold in the 1950's clearly showing the iron kettle prop and the cooking utensils over an open fire.

(Left) The contents of the cooking pot are revealed!

21

Waiting for his dinner! The larger sticks in the fire are placed like the spokes of a wheel so that the air runs between them and gives a better, hotter fire.

Tradesman's cart, highly ornate and usually used in conjunction with the caravan as a runabout and work vehicle and whilst on a journey. Jack won't be doing a lot with all that snow about!

some draught to start it off. A large cast-iron pan with a lid forms the basis of all Gypsy cooking and the raw food is prepared and tied in separate little muslin bags. Water is added to the pot first and heated over the flames and the ingredients are added in order of cooking times. Slow cooking items are added first and the quicker cooking items later so that they can all be removed and eaten at the same time when ready. The whole pot and contents are suspended from a bent iron rod driven into the ground and positioned over the fire at the desired height. This also doubles up to hold the kettle if another iron is not available. Meals are cooked and eaten in the late afternoon when the day's work is completed and the women have been able to obtain supplies from the shops. Special meals are prepared in the same way but with a little extra care and effort. For example at Christmas time all the stops are pulled out to make the meal a special occasion. The very best tablecloth, linen and crockery would be brought out and the cooking most likely done in the waggon because at this time of year the weather may not be too favourable outside.

Travellers are not very adventurous in their eating habits and where possible use natural meat and vegetables. Rabbit, game birds and fish are supplemented with bought bacon and cheap lamb joints that can be boiled or fried, as these are the only two ways to cook over a wood fire.

Purchases from the village shop would include white crusty bread, tea, sugar, stock cubes, self-raising flour, suet, lard, butter, cheese, eggs, matches, candles and special items like cakes, jelly, and tins of rice pudding for afters. The tea was nearly always taken very sweet and with condensed milk added. Even if fresh milk was available the longer-lasting tinned variety was the most popular. Now that most families live in smart modern trailers that usually contain a fridge or deep freeze many different types of foodstuff can be stored so the above-mentioned items may appear very basic and outdated today.

The menu and recipes would have been handed down from mother to daughter and would be fairly traditional with the exception of the Christmas fare. Goose was the bird most chosen for this meal as it could be the acting watchdog round the camp and could even walk along the route with the Gypsies, eating as it went. It was always given extra and special food for the latter part of its life, like corn and leftovers, to provide extra flavour. When cooked the stuffing would comprise potatoes, goose liver, apples, sage, mushrooms, thyme, parsley, lemon thyme, pepper, salt and eggs. Green beans, jacket potatoes and turnip with apple sauce would complement the meal, followed by a light sweet and homemade wine from the hedgerow like elderberry or apple. The meal would be complete.

After the meal, before the advent of the television set wired up to the car battery, the family sat around the fire drinking tea and smoking their 'baccy.' Some of the men might be able to play the violin or mouth organ and would get the family to join in a sing-song. Modern tunes of the day or more traditional Romany songs passed down through the generations would be sung depending on what sort of a mood the company was in. In the case of the Romany songs these tended to be sung by individual families and were not generally shared. If a guest was included round the fire when songs were being sung he would not repeat these when he was at his own fire or in the company of others as they would know where he had learned them. Only after many such visits over a period of years would the friendship develop sufficiently to allow the transfer of certain family songs outside the immediate circle.

If near a village or town the men might have a couple of hours at the public house before returning home to the women and children in their caravans, first seeing that the horses were well tied up and in no danger to themselves or others, and that the fire ashes had been carefully banked up into a pyramid with a large flat log on the top to stop any rain damping it out. If rain fell during the night the drops hit the wood ash and cascaded down the sides of the pyramid and did not put out the heart of the fire, which could then be easily rekindled in the morning.

One old traveller tells of a further use for the wood fire. To keep one step ahead of the gamekeeper if a pheasant accidentally came to hand he would heat a large cooking pot filled with sand over the open fire. Then he would gut and bury the bird in the sand complete with feathers, also sticking in a few lengths of ash or willow so that their ends softened when heated. The purpose of this exercise was twofold. Firstly the hot sand cooked the bird and when this was done the feathers and the outside skin were peeled off and thrown onto the fire to remove the evidence. The idea of the sticks was the second reason so that he would be able to tell the gamekeeper, if caught, that he was only making walking sticks and bending the handles.

Pig-meat formed an important part of the Romany diet if it was available. Bacon would be purchased from the shops on their journeys but fresh meat was harder to come by. In days gone by, and not heard of today due to people's mobility and the advent of fridges and freezers in the modern trailers, the art of catching pigs with a mineral called 'drab' is now almost folk lore.

Drab is actually witherite in its natural crystal state, or to use its proper name Barium Carbonate, and was used by the Gypsies to feed to pigs making them appear dead. The farmer would willingly give these supposed 'dead' animals away and the pig would either recover or be killed and then cooked and eaten.

The yellow/green mineral was heated to break it down and was then powdered prior to being used. Shropshire was the main source of this fairly rare mineral. The Welsh travellers had a supply near to Hollywell. Others purchased theirs from travellers at fairs and horse sales during the year for use when needed.

Whilst the material and the technique was mainly practised in the South of England because of its availability, it was not entirely unknown in Yorkshire. Visitors to Brough Hill Fair could obtain supplies and it was never really known if the 'drab' was found locally or if it was imported from the known areas. Possibly the nearest local findings were just outside Hexham where there were remains of lead mine-workings. When this mine was re-opened in the 1840's until the First World War witherite had been its main product. From Brough Hill Fair to the October Hull Fair which directly followed it drab could be carried for re-sale. Barium Carbonate can be obtained from chemists and they may have been the main suppliers in the North of England.

The technique used to administer drab was to cut a hole in a potato or an apple, insert the powder, then replace the plug to remove all traces. The size of the amount given depended very much on the size of the animal but usually the quantity that could rest on the top of an old penny would suffice. The animal might vomit, foam at the mouth, with internal colic and due to its sickly appearance the farmer considered he was well rid of it before it infected the whole herd. To the Romany the head and internal organs were rejected but all the other parts would have been eaten without any ill effect.

There is mention in a very old medical journal of nineteen patients requiring hospital treatment after eating sausages, for diarrhoea, vomiting, weakness, dryness of mouth, paralysis, headaches etc. It could be that travellers had used drab on a pig and then sold it to a local butcher who in turn made it up into sausages with these unfortunate results.

The desire to survive by their wits like pig killing, poaching and other slightly dubious enterprises is always accompanied by the desire to keep within the law unless circumstances decreed otherwise.

Hawking, selling small items door to door by the womenfolk, is the main way of obtaining funds. Small things like pins, pencils, ribbons, elastic, cottons, brushes are purchased in the towns and sold at a small profit from the basket. The items themselves would not show a big profit but the Gypsy women might manage to extract a little food or articles of cast-off clothing from the householder as well, and all these added to the daily takings when re-sold. At the end of the day the waggon would be parked a little way outside the village and the spoils of the day shared by all the family. In the case of clothes the grown-ups and children alike selected suitable items for themselves and paraded around in the firelight showing off their latest acquisitions.

Times are changing so fast now that many of these customs are nearly extinct. The small saleable goods like the traditional clothes peg are now bought from the nearest supermarket when not so long ago the menfolk made them whilst the women were out 'calling.' Made from hazel or willow sticks the

(Left) Gypsy lady making 'Chrysanthemums' from the elder bush stalks by shaving the wood with a sharp knife. When the shavings dry they curl, giving the effect of a flower. Sometimes dipped in vegetable colour to give variety. With a little green added they are sold round the houses.

(Below) Don, Sooty and friends at Fryton Lane End, near Hovingham, North Yorkshire, in the hot summer of 1976 ready for the start of a journey.

pegs passed down a sort of human production line. Three or four men could complete a gross an hour by stripping off the bark, cutting to length, tinning the end, splitting and 'throating,' each man doing one operation and then passing it on to the next till the peg was complete.

When out 'calling' the women knew the good houses where they were welcome for a cup of tea and a chat and where they were able to read a palm, or tell a fortune. Even so they were very superstitious and would never call on certain days or at certain times considered unlucky.

Other signs were taken note of and good and bad omens followed. For instance if the hair was cut at the time of the new moon this would give good fortune. Conversely, Gypsies would never rake out a coal or wood fire as this was said to be unlucky. If a lump of coal was in their path they would pick it up to be sure of success.

The position of the bed head was considered significant and the house-holders might be asked if their bed head was at the west. If so they would be told that they may travel; if in the east, riches might result; to the north a short life, and to the south a long one.

This was all very awe-inspiring for the country or town people, who did not quite know what to make of these dark-skinned visitors to their homes.

To find a horseshoe would bring luck as everyone knows but if you were to lose it or give it away your luck might also disappear.

Many travellers sadly have met an untimely end by the natural elements of fire, water or lightning. Even though some have been killed by direct flashes of lightning, it is said that it would never strike anyone who is asleep; also that a house will not be hit if a fire is burning in the grate.

Water and the accident of drowning feature in the Romany way of life, as water for them, like us, is a most essential item of everyday life. Whereas our supply comes out of the tap courtesy of the local water board, the traveller has to find his and fill cans from running water, when many a tragedy has happened. Water should never be added to a jug already containing water as this promotes mischief and misunderstanding.

The Gypsy has a very great respect for the facets of nature and knows that everything is placed on this earth for a good reason and should not be abused.

It is interesting to note that a Gypsy who leaves the open air and freedom of the highways and byeways for the town life can become a changed person in a very short time. Somehow the sparkle goes out of his nature and he may be dull and uninteresting. His nature, dress and manner may change and unless he manages to return to his former freedom of the open road, he is lost.

In Yorkshire there are a few groups of travellers who seem to be partly on the road and partly dependent on the towns and the state for their livelihood. They are set between two stools and belong neither to the world of the house-dweller nor the true Romany. They may be part Romany stock but they have succumbed to the modern way of life, portable wireless sets and televisions wired into car batteries all spoiling their romantic image.

Times are changing, and the past will never be the same again either for us, the non-Gypsy, or the Gypsies themselves. They need the open road to be happy and content; if only they could be left in peace.

Catastrophe on Beggars Bridge, Glaisdale, North Yorkshire, in the early 1900's. A two-horse Bow-top type waggon where the leading horse has jumped over the parapet with the second horse still suspended in its harness.

A Bow-top caravan with the Vale of Pickering as a backdrop. This is more of a 'Horse Shoe' shaped bow, being slightly flattened at the apex.

CHAPTER TWO

YORKSHIRE FAIRS

An area the size of Yorkshire had its families that travelled from one fair to another during the summer months, making each one a place to conduct business and also to meet up with old friends and have a few days rest. During the different seasons of the year they moved about an area to obtain work and while the winter months were quiet the spring, summer and autumn found plenty for them to occupy their time.

Being able to organise journeys on an annual basis was one of the joys of travelling as arrangements could be made in advance and events looked forward to from one year to the next.

A major part of the Gypsies' enjoyment was the horse fairs. Though only taking up about one month in the year all told, they provided the chance to meet friends and relations for a few days without the need to be moved on.

Many of these fairs were set up by Royal Charter and gave permission for trading during the duration of the fair. As long as the peace was kept they provided a safe haven for a few days.

Throughout Yorkshire, towns and villages all held small one-day fairs at some time during the year but the main ones were Yarm, Lee Gap, Topcliffe, Seamer, Boroughbridge, Hull and to a lesser extent Malton.

Yarm Fair

Yarm Fair, now in the Cleveland area, must be one of the oldest as it is claimed to be an 800-year-old charter fair held in October each year. Following the tradition first started in the early 19th Century the Riding of the Fair takes place on a Saturday in October which is the last day of the three-day event. Over the years the proclamation has been read by the Lord of the Manor and now by the Chairman of the Weigh & Tolls Committee as successor to the Lord of the Manor. It was the custom to make the reading from a horse-drawn vehicle in four positions off the large market-square, preceded by a fanfare from the hornblower in grey topper, morning suit and lace cuffs, on a posthorn made in 1397.

One problem with this fair is that roundabouts and side stalls are now taking over from the original cattle, sheep and horse fair and pushing the smaller Gypsy contingent into the River Leven. The old photographs show how cattle were held in open fronted pens at each side of the square by the houses. A man was positioned at the open end and would allow the animals to come out and parade about if a prospective buyer so wished.

The days when 500 tons, yes tons, of cheese were sold during the Fair before

Middlesbrough existed are chronicled in a remarkable and well-preserved Yorkshire Directory published about 1822.

Gypsies and their horse-drawn caravans provided a lot of interest at the Stockton end of the square, reading palms, telling fortunes and selling horses and ponies. These animals would be cantered along the roadway for all to see and some brisk deals would be completed with the traditional hand slap during the three-day fair.

Gradually as time passed and the flow of traffic greatly increased, the running of horses in the main street has proved to be a traffic hazard. As the showmen have augmented the size and style of their machinery so they have taken more and more of the ground space. Older travellers say that formerly they had the ground from the river bridge to the toilet block in the centre of the square and the showmen had the other half. Today the Gypsies have a very small area at the bridge end on the side of the cobbled road and next to the footpath.

In October 1961 there were 40 caravans in the cobbled high street by late afternoon but only eight were horse-drawn. In 1962 it proved to be a very quiet year, the slackest for thirty years, according to some of the older travellers. Trade was down and the local auctioneer reported that the horse sales were very slow with no-one showing interest.

In 1973 the famous horse sales were held outside the parish for the first time in living memory, because the date clashed with the local cattle market. All selling was conducted four miles away at the Stockton Cattle Market.

October 1979 saw the end of selling sheep and cattle by Messrs. R. & W. Hedley, the Yarm auctioneers, because the fair day was changed to Saturday. A

Yarm Fair in 1916. This photograph shows the effect the Great War had on attendances.

(Left) A 1930's group at Yarm Fair enjoying a cup of tea prepared over the open fire on the cobblestones.

(Below) The Gypsy end of Yarm Fair nearest the rail and river bridges in the Market Place at the turn of this century.

31

report in the "Northern Echo" of this year quotes Mr. Fred Rigg, the Yarm Parish Council Chairman, as saying that the fair will one day lose its Gypsy flavour. His memory from childhood was of a deal of congestion on the cobbles, of smokey fires, and opening his shop in the morning to find horse manure on the doorstep, horses tied to the lamp posts (even children tied to lamp posts) and horses being put through their paces, racing up and down the High Street.

In 1980 after a lapse of about twenty years, the Gypsies, under the leadership of Lawrence Wood, intended to run horses up and down Yarm High Street to bring an atmosphere back to the event. This may have flouted the law, but an offence would only be committed if an obstruction was caused; at least it showed that Yarm was originally a Gypsy and animal fair. As things turned out the police gave a special dispensation for half an hour to allow the horses to be trotted.

By 1985 the rent for traditional carts had increased from £2 to £7.50 with a charge of £20 for a vehicle-pulled trailer compared to £10 the previous year. According to the travellers the Yarm charges were now on a par with Appleby Horse Fair despite the latter being a far longer and better fair; also the horses could no longer be trotted to advantage in the street at Yarm.

The Gypsies' argument is that there is no mention in the original charter of the showmen but it does mention the sale of horses, sheep and cattle. Due to a

Gypsy fortune teller Mrs. Tilley Wood. She has attended most of the Fairs in Yorkshire over a fifty year period and is seen here at Yarm Fair reading a palm in 1984.

Lawrence Wood and his daughter Nation, aged three, outside their caravan in Yarm Market Place during Fair week in 1985.

few younger energetic travellers, the Gypsies were starting to stand up for themselves and talks now take place with the Yarm Parish Council with representatives of the Gypsies being invited to attend.

Suggestions have been made that old land where the weekly cattle market took place should be used for the parking of trailer caravans and the grazing and trotting of horses but this is off the main road and might not be viable. People who attend might not see them at the back of the main market place, tucked under the shadow of the railway viaduct.

The town shopkeepers in Yarm are not altogether happy with the Fair because they claim to be losing three days' trading. They argue that their businesses are hemmed in by trailers, machines, caravans and people. It would seem though that all these extra people should bring added prosperity to the town for these few days, but the Yarm Chamber of Trade does not agree and they may know best.

The future for this fair may be brighter, especially if the younger travellers like Lawrence Wood continue to press for what they see, and the original Charter says, is a Gypsy Fair.

Lee Gap Fair

Lee Gap Fair at Woodkirk in the West Riding owes its origin to a Charter granted by Henry I to the Augustinian Canons of Nostell Priory to whom the Church of Woodkirk (West Ardsley) was given by the Second Earl De Warenne at the beginning of the 12th Century.

This Charter granted to the Canons the right to hold two fairs annually, on the 15th of August and on the 8th of September. It was confirmed when the Gregorian calendar was adopted in 1752 and the dates were set back to August 24th and September 17th, on which dates it continues to be held. Charters were granted only by the King and were regarded as a privilege by those who received them. The owners of the grant received their income from the fees that they charged stallholders.

Not only horses were sold at Lee Gap, but also salted meat and fish, cheeses, wines, cloth and silk, furs, spices and all things needed for everyday use.

Getting to the Fair before the roads were made up as we know them today proved to be a hazardous business and groups of people and horses and carts tended to travel together for protection over the narrow, bumpy roads.

A fair, presumably the Lee Gap Fair, is mentioned in the Court Rolls of the Manor of Wakefield in November 1306 and as these records show a riotous time was had by all. There were many cases of theft, fights and generally rowdy behaviour. In 1315 a stall was overturned and the owner claimed the loss of 209 gallons of beer priced at two shillings and six pence!

By 1656 this fair had become a great cloth market, clashing with the newly opened cloth market at Wakefield. There was a petition sent to the Lord Protector (Oliver Cromwell) that the latter should be closed but nothing was ever done.

The name was changed from Woodkirk Fair to Lee Gap Fair after the dissolution of the Monasteries, when Nostell Priory was granted to Dr. Leigh from whom the fair later took its name.

In 1871 the fair was held on the top and side of a hill east of the Church and not far from an older site called Fair Steads field. By 1935 it was a smaller collection of a few Welsh ponies and farm livestock — nothing like its previous size. No side stalls selling all manner of goods have been seen since.

During the last forty or fifty years all the fields that used to be filled with Gypsy caravans and horses have now been built on so the fair is limited to one field only, but at least it continues.

A report in the local paper, the 'Express,' dated 1927 states: "The fair is a declining institution. One need not be very old to realise how steadily it delines — and yet it never dies."

Seamer Fair

King Richard II granted the Charter for Seamer Fair to Henry Percy Duke of Northumberland, giving authority for a market to be held at Seamer each Monday and for a fair of a week's duration (excluding Sundays) to commence on the feast of St. Martin provided that it did not interfere with neighbouring markets and fairs that had already been established (i.e. Scarborough, Brompton, Filey and Sherburn).

There was a Pie Powder Court, as at Malton's Michaelmas Fair, which would deal with any disputes about sales. Permission was given for any householder to open for the fair as an ale house if he displayed the branch of a tree above his door. As many as twenty houses would brew their own beer and sell it at the fair.

The original date for the fair was July 4th but in 1752 when the Gregorian calendar was adopted eleven days were taken out of the calendar; therefore today's fair is proclaimed on July 15th.

There is still a Monday market held every week at Crossgates, Seamer, and the former horse fair is now mainly the reading of the Charter and the scattering of coins on the green by the Lord of the Manor of Seamer. A copy of the Charter is held by the present Lord and Lady of the Manor, Mr. and Mrs. Andrew Green, and another by the Hull Museum with the original being in the British Museum.

At 11.50 a.m. on July the 15th the Charter is read at various points in the village and a crier first shouts 'Oyez, Oyez, Oyez,' to gain attention and then a mounted representative reads:

"Whereas King Richard, the second, on the 11th November in the sixth year of his reign in the year of our Lord one thousand three hundred and thirty seven, did grant unto the Lords of this Manor and their heirs for ever, one fair yearly to be kept in the said Manor upon the fourth day of July being St. Martin's Day and so to continue for the space of seven days, by virtue of which grant and confirmation thereof from time to time.

"We do openly proclaim, publish and declare, that this Fair, beginning on the fifteenth day of July and so for seven days following, except the Lord's Day it shall and may be lawful for all and every person and persons resorting to this fair to buy, sell, bargain or deal for any lawful goods, wares, merchandise, horses, geldings, mares, colts, fillies, beasts, sheep and any other cattle

The opening of Seamer Fair, about 1920.

whatsoever, paying unto the Lord of the Manor by his officers appointed to receive the same pollage, package, stallage, standage, and other duties belonging to him for the same.

"And we do in the Queen's Majesty's name strictly charge and command all manner of persons whatsoever coming and reporting to this fair, and in the end so to depart.

"God save the Queen and the Lord of the Manor."

The sixth year of the reign of King Richard II (1377-1399) must be 1383 and so the one so solemnly announced of 1337 must be incorrect. How this error occurred no-one knows; perhaps the original was misplaced and another rewritten from memory, or copied wrongly from another document.

Within living memory, the Gypsies would have camped on the side of the A64 between the trees on the right hand side from Malton to Scarborough for three days. The Fair started with six days, then went to three and is now only one day. Others were parked on the back lane. They always had a fire on the green and water was obtained with permission from farm buildings on the other side of the main road. This was the period between the two world wars. A popular place for caravans was also in the field next to the Church.

A report of 1890 states that there was an exceedingly large supply of horses and ponies, but beasts were scarce. Good prices were realised in all classes. The demand for carthorses was great, with buyers coming from all parts of the country. Carthorses realised from £15 to £60, harness horses from £30 to £40

36

and ponies, of which there were nearly one hundred, from £10 to £20. Compare this report with the one for 1911 which said that there were a good number of horses shown, but these were perhaps below the average of the standard of previous years. Carthorses were selling from £15 to £45 and lighter horses from £20 to £35. The report for this year goes on to note that the attendance at the fair was not large, due to the exceptionally fine weather, to the fact that the harvesting operations were in progress, and that it was held on a Saturday.

It was on the Saturday of this 1911 fair that the worst troubles and events in its long history occurred. From enquiries made at the time from several persons in Seamer who witnessed the affray it would appear that at eight o'clock in the evening two Seamer men named Baker and Jim Young entered the Londesborough Arms. Several potters (because they traditionally sold crockery) or Gypsies visiting the fair whose caravans were in the field in the village were having a sing-song. The Seamer men were talking together and the potters called for order. Apparently the villagers did not comply and one of the potters thereupon struck Baker a blow in the face. Baker did not retaliate, but Young struck the potter back again. A general scuffle ensued in the room. The police were sent for and the potters ejected, while the Seamer men, who threatened to come out after them, were tactfully induced to remain at the house in order to avert further trouble. The potters allowed themselves to be conducted to their caravans, and for a time peace was restored.

At about half-past ten, when the public house had closed, a body of forty or fifty villagers proceeded towards the potters' camp. On the way they met a man called Smith, one of the best known of the camp of potters, and a scuffle took place, but Smith got away to his caravan. Inflamed, the villagers apparently armed themselves with hedge stakes and proceeded to the Manor Field where the potters' camp was situated. Here they commenced to belabour the caravans with hedge stakes, and one of the potters asserts, with what truth cannot be said, that he was pulled forcibly out of bed and struck.

By all reports the potters were not slow to take up the battle with the villagers, at whom they hurled hot cinders, bricks, and any missiles which came to hand. Ultimately about seven or eight men, backed by about a dozen of their womenfolk and armed with iron bars, made an ugly rush at the villagers, who did not stand to meet the attack, but beat a retreat. It was said at this stage that the police, who had been hurriedly sent for, arrived on the scene, and probably prevented more serious consequences. As it was Thomas Pearson, a farmer from Meats Farm, and two other men, named James Shields, a platelayer from Long Lane Crossing, and Robert Walker, were quietly walking homewards just as the crowd was retreating, and not knowing the danger there was, as they had not been taking part in the affray, became exposed to the fury of the potters. Whether or not the potters took them for part of the gang that had attacked the camp it is impossible to say, but they were furiously assailed with iron bars. The point at which this occurred was on the road under a dense row of trees skirting the roadside at the Manor Field. The darkness of the night was intensified by the shade of the trees and exactly what took place is very uncertain.

What is quite clear is that as soon as P.C. Mail from Seamer and P.C.

Bromley from Cayton, who had been left in the village, had got the potters safely back into the Manor Field again, they found Pearson lying unconscious with a severe cut on the top of his head. He was conveyed to the Londesborough Arms and remained unconscious all night, recovering on Sunday morning.

Shields was suffering from a bad cut on the head which required seven stitches. He was taken unconscious to the Londesborough Arms. He remained there until Sunday when, having no fixed address, he was taken to Scarborough Hospital.

A youth named Fred Keld of Seamer, who was one of the crowd of villagers, sustained a broken collar bone. A Seamer man named Joe Milow, who was also one of the crowd, suffered from a number of bruises from being kicked, and P.C. Bromley received a heavy blow across the shoulders from a stick. None of the potters sustained any serious injury; indeed, the only injury appears to have been to a man sustaining a cut on the nose and two black eyes. Dr. Candler Hope was sent for and attended to the injured man.

After the affray there were no further outbreaks, but the police kept a careful watch all night to prevent any recurrence of the trouble.

The potters left on Sunday morning, their names having been taken, but it was impossible to say whether court proceedings would be the outcome. No arrest was made and on the Monday Seamer was as calm and peaceful as usual and no-one could have imagined that so recently there had been such riotous scenes and bloodshed.

Bringing the story up to date, eighty-seven-year-old Mr. J. W. Dawson can recall as a small boy what he calls 'deep trouble' between the Gypsies and the locals, all more or less drunk. His uncle rushed into his grandfather, borrowed his gun and rushed out again, but he understood the police to have intervened and a riot was avoided. He was rushed off to bed, but could not sleep because of all the activity. He says that the ground below the Vicarage and down to Ratten Row was packed with caravans and fires, as was the other side of the road and the whole of Ratten Row itself.

During the day things were very busy as horses with carts were driven furiously up and down the village street, put through their best paces to promote a sale.

One of the village shopkeepers, the previously mentioned Mr. Dawson, pointed out that the task of the shopkeepers was unenviable as the Gypsies flocked into the premises for food and sometimes they were none too honest. Four or five would ask for the same thing at once to baffle the assistant and if careful watch wasn't kept some things landed into their baskets without payment. If he offered cheap bacon fat-ends or stale bacon, perhaps four or five pounds for a shilling (5p), they would say that they only had sixpence (2½p).

After the First World War in 1922, a Mr. Louis Ferrari of Leeds purchased the Manorial rights of the reputed Manor of Seamer at an auction for £50. The fair at this time, due to the war, had really fallen off and the price of a top quality horse was £30 for a class that would have realised £120 five years earlier.

The motor car was also blamed because it was taking over from the horse which had been the main reason for the fair. Scarborough buyers would purchase horses for hauling herring from the harbour to the station but this trade was also in decline.

By 1930 a Mr. A. L. Rhodes from Doncaster was Lord of the Manor of Seamer and it was thought that the tradition still carried out today of throwing pennies for the children was started by him. In this year there was once again a fairly serious clash with locals and visitors to the fair, not as bad as previously but nevertheless showing that ill feeling was still there between the two parties.

Fancy dress, side shows, carnival sports and dance were all added attractions by the mid 1930's and the spirit of the fair seemed to be reviving. A marquee was erected and a dance was well attended to enjoy the music of the Corona Band.

It was reported at the time of these added attractions in the mid 1930's that members of the Romany tribe were congregated at the far end of the village and creating considerable interest, as the question of their camping sites was still a debatable topic.

The fair today is only a small one in the village, though the fatstock market still prospers in the capable hands of the Malton auctioneers Messrs. Boulton & Cooper Ltd., themselves founded in 1801. The local travellers, however, now seem determined to revive its fortunes and the future does look better.

Topcliffe Fair

Topcliffe Fair was granted a Royal Charter in 1343 and was held for hundreds of years until it finally ended in 1970 due to the withdrawal of the charter. On the 16th of March 1970 a letter was received by the Parish Council from the Right Honourable James Callaghan M.P. which effectively finished off the fair, and read as follows:

Home Office,
Whitehall,
London, S.W.1.

16th March, 1970

Dear Sirs,

Whereas a representation was made to me as Secretary of State for the Home Department by Thirsk Rural District Council in January 1969, that it would be for the convenience and advantage of the public that the fair held annually in the village of Topcliffe, in the County of Yorkshire should be abolished;

And whereas notice of the said representation, and of the time, when the same would be taken into consideration has been duly published in pursuance of the Fairs Act 1871 (a);

And whereas it appears to me after considering the said representation that it would be for the convenience and advantage of the public that the said fair should be abolished;

And whereas the owner for the time being has consented in writing to the abolition;

Now therefore, I the Right Honourable James Callaghan, M.P., one of Her Majesty's Principal Secretaries of State, in exercise of the powers conferred upon me by section three of the Fairs Act 1871, do hereby order that the fair which has been held annually in the Village of Topcliffe in the County of Yorkshire shall be abolished.

Signed JAMES CALLAGHAN

Topcliffe is situated near Thirsk in the North Riding of Yorkshire and had been a popular horse fair for many years. Caravans had been parked beside the River Swale for three days each July with the Gypsies supplying the local farmers with their work horses.

Traditionally with a horse fair there are also other produce stalls and extra attractions but there is no mention of these with Topcliffe Fair.

Due to continual bad behaviour and the farmers' grass fields being grazed without permission, the villagers got fed up with the fair. The final straw for them was when a firearm was discharged and it looked as though things were going to get out of hand. Eighty villagers called a meeting and voted against the fair continuing and the Lord of the Manor, Lord Leaconfield, agreed to petition the Home Secretary for the withdrawal of the Charter. Thirsk Rural District Council also supported this suggestion and the Topcliffe councillors submitted a proposal to have the fair stopped.

Before this turn of events, it is reported in 1961 that there were seventy Gypsy caravans parked in the Upper and Lower fields at the fair. Eleven were ordinary bow-tops, two square-tops, twenty-nine 'open-lots,' two accommodations, two William Wright bow-tops, and twenty-four modern living trailers. This gives a good selection of caravan types but even so there were no examples of the larger Reading or Burton type of vehicles. Today, about twenty-five years later, this show of caravans no longer takes place. Vehicles like these are now hardly ever made and in view of the tradition that the caravan is burnt on the death of the owner, they are becoming extremely scarce.

Topcliffe, like all fairs, was a meeting place where friends and families could see each other once a year and swap stories and complete deals. A few years ago one family visited Topcliffe with a couple of the Romany lurcher dogs and unfortunately one died. So much was thought of this animal that it was buried in a 'safe' field where it would not be disturbed by development or ploughing and each time the family passed the site they tidied the grave and eventually planted a weeping willow tree on the spot.

A nice testimony to a once great fair could be a few lines written by an anonymous eighteenth century poet:

> The Law locks up the man or woman
> Who steals the goose from off the common
> But lets the greater villain loose
> Who steels the common off the goose.

Malton Michaelmas Fair

Malton Michaelmas Fair is held for two days in the autumn each year. Whilst not actually a Royal Charter fair (because a document cannot be found) this event has altered its dates over the last few years to suit the market trading patterns of the day.

(Top) The German Gypsies, who seemed to create havoc throughout Great Britain for a three-year period, seen here encamped at Old Malton, North Yorkshire, for Michaelmas Fair on October 11th, 1906. Wherever they went they had their photograph taken in a group with the local police constables.

(Bottom) Malton Market Square outside St. Michael's Church showing the attendance of the November fairground rides and what looks like a Church Parade in the early 1920's.

The town crier still officially opens the fair from the Market Place, the cattle market and the show field at Pasture Lane, ringing a bell and reading:

"Oyez! Oyez! Oyez! Notice is hereby given that the Right Honourable Earl Fitzwilliam Lord of this Manor, doth hereby declare the fair open for the space of two holidays. From the rising to the setting of the sun. For the sale and exchange of all classes of merchandise. Those attending are charged to keep the peace and good order throughout the fair. A court of piepowder will be held in the market for the settling of all disputes and grievances. God save the Queen and the Lord of this Manor."

At the Michaelmas Fair of October 1906 a feature was the presence of German Gypsies intent on horse dealing. But they left on Saturday morning. They really wished to stay over until Sunday, but Superintendent Heald gave them peremptory orders to march. They got off about half past nine in the morning, making their way to Yarm Fair. Going through Ampleforth on Sunday morning the farmers and villagers armed themselves with sticks and guns and drove them on though not without some difficulty. One of the Gypsies threatened a man with an axe, but a gun presented at him induced the King of the Gypsies to give the order to move out, which they did.

Many of the fairs in Yorkshire received a visit from this band of about fifty German Gypsies. They were a very mixed group of men, women and children travelling the whole of Great Britain during a two-year period. They appeared in 1905 and stayed by all reports until 1907 when they returned to their native Germany. Never popular, mainly because of their unkempt appearance, and maybe sometimes their lack of the English language to make their needs known, they were hounded from village to village. They had a liking for having their photograph taken and many exist over this period in different parts of the country showing their group usually with a couple of local policemen standing at the edge. It cannot have been a very friendly experience for them and one would surmise that they were glad to return to their homeland.

For many years the Michaelmas Fair at Malton attracted the Gypsy dealer for the sale of horses as well as the sale of cattle and sheep. Horses would run in front of the Spotted Cow Inn where the final details of any sale were conducted over a pint or two of beer.

In the 1980's this tradition finally came to an end with the only local traveller family who bothered to bring any horses ceasing to do so.

In place of this fair local auctioneers have organised a monthly sale in the cattle market of horses and harness, which is well attended by the dealers and public from a wide area. Though the interest today is mainly for the riding horse and pony there is still trade to be done.

Barnaby Fair (Boroughbridge)

Charles the First granted the charter for this fair in 1622 enabling people to sell ale on "Barnaby Day.' Lemon curd tarts were baked specially during the fair fortnight period, earlier this century, and called 'Barnaby Tarts.'

In the second week the roundabouts and swings came into the bottom square in Boroughbridge with 'Aunt Sallies' and stalls of all different kinds.

Years ago the main horse fair was in the short street leading into the Market

Place. There was a good run from there to the main road and back for the horses to be put through their paces. Traditionally following Appleby Fair in June, this is where the Gypsy prefers to conduct his more serious business. Appleby he regards as a social gathering whereas here he can arrange deals away from the interested gaze of the general public. Once a two-week event, but now only held for one day because of rowdy troublemakers in the past, the horse sales are run on an organised basis by a local firm of auctioneers. Very close to the main A1 road at Boroughbridge, the selling field was next to Kelly's Café but now the café is a large supermarket and the field has houses built in it.

The Gypsy has tried to find a sympathetic ear and the loan of a suitable field to no avail. Once again due to the loutish behaviour of the few, the farmers and landowners in the area just do not want to know and one cannot blame them for that. One or two pub landlords have offered the use of their car parks but in the main these are totally unsuitable and are highly dangerous because of the lack of room for both men and horses. The slightest upset with the horses presents a danger to all concerned.

Hull Fair

Hull Fair has had many special Charters over the years. Records go back as far as the year 1278 when the Abbot of Meaux in Holderness, realising the need for better facilities for buying and selling local goods, founded a fair. At this time when people could not travel long distances to purchase their needs, the fairs had to be brought to them. This was a once-a-year chance for the people to purchase what they required to last them until the fair returned again. Various dates and length of duration were recorded in these very early days until Hull was made a free borough by Edward I in April 1299 and all the liberties and customs were carried on.

Over the last two hundred years the fair has been reduced to only six working days until 1952 when an additional Saturday was added to the fair's duration, starting on the Saturday nearest to the 10th October.

From the earliest days of the fair nothing was actually organised. Stalls were erected for the sale of produce wherever there was a space and entertainment in the form of crude plays was performed. Hull was never really a horse fair throughout its history even though cattle, goats and sheep were offered for sale from its earliest days. Eventually the animal sales were conducted in outside town markets like Driffield and the fairground side of the fair continued and increased. From 1966 to 1975, after a seventeen-year lapse, there were attempts to revive the horse fair, but with only a dozen or so animals being offered for sale it fell through. In the years when horses were being sold the fairground people did most of the dealing and not the Gypsies as may have been expected. They required many horses to transport their rides from one location to another, sometimes as many as twenty-five horses to pull one show.

In the early 16th Century the fair established a court of 'Pie-Powder,' as did Malton and Seamer. This court was set up to see justice for both buyer and seller and disputes of all types could be settled on the spot. The name is thought to derive from the French 'Pied Purdreaux,' a pedlar who frequented fairs. Now any disputes or court actions are dealt with by the City's magistrates.

Hull Fair was presumed to have been held in its earliest days outside the walls of the Church which stood on the site of the old Holy Trinity Church. The local traders and merchants sold wool, grain, cloth and lead, purchasing in exchange from foreign traders furs, cloths, wine, hops and spices for curing meat.

From the Crown and the town authorities' point of view the fair was important for raising large revenues from rents and tolls charged to the stall holders and visitors.

In 1888 the fair moved to its present Walton Street site. Local councillors of the day hoped the move would put an end to the fair once and for all as it was on the outskirts of the town. However, once it managed to survive the move, the council took some pride in the fairground aspect of it and made up for their former neglect by assisting all they could.

From the start at Walton Street, the Markets and Abattoirs Committee was appointed to oversee the fair, a function now carried out by the Leisure Services Committee. Special trains and ferries had to be laid on at the time of the fair to cope with the additional interest.

In 1907 the Walton Street ground was extended from six to twelve acres making it the largest in the country at that time. 1922 saw the site filled in with clinker and then in 1961 it was properly tarmacked. Residents of Walton Street let out their front gardens to stall holders for an agreed rent to compensate them for the noise and litter they had to suffer for the fair's duration. Also because of fire regulations they had to sleep in their downstairs' rooms.

In 1923, also for fire safety, naked flames known as naptha lamps were prohibited and the Edison electric light was substituted. Due to an accident in 1928 when a night warden dropped his gas lamp and destroyed a section of toy stalls, fire-fighting equipment and water points were set up. Eventually in 1938 the street became the first fairground in the country to give showmen access to the city's main electricity supply.

The horses have gone now and the main entertainment is the modern fairground rides but some old-fashioned attractions can still be seen. The coconut shies, toffee apples, brandy snaps, candyfloss are all to be had from stalls and side shows. Fortune-telling booths and caravans are manned by the Gypsies who love the hassle and colour of a fair like this to attract customers.

Nowadays other facilities provided on site are telephones, refuse collections, meal waggons, St. John's Ambulancemen and even employees of the Social Services Department who check on the welfare of the showmen! The St. John's Ambulancemen have been attending the fair regularly for one hundred years and certainly provide a very worthwhile service.

The planning of the fair starts in January each year when the sites and parking spaces are allocated. As this is a fair vetted by the Showmen's Guild they ensure that everything runs smoothly when the fair arrives in October

It is certainly an unusual and spectacular event and one wonders in this modern age how long it can continue. With the showpeople depending on the money from this fair seeing them over the winter months and the sites to operate from becoming fewer, only time will tell.

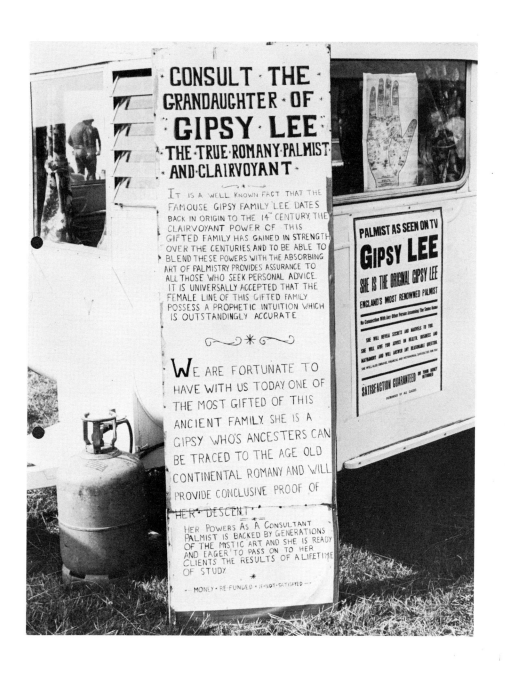

Typical palmistry sign outside a modern trailer at a show. Whilst some are very ornate the wording is always similar.

CHAPTER THREE

BROUGH HILL AND APPLEBY FAIRS

Brough Hill Fair and Appleby Fair must be included in any record of Yorkshire Gypsy fairs as they are the two largest and most popular in the North of England and attended by Gypsies from all over the country, including many from Yorkshire.

Now in Cumbria, late of Westmorland, the town of Appleby sits astride the meandering river Eden. Each half of the town is linked by an old arched stone roadbridge.

Being chartered fairs for the sale of livestock, produce, clothing and anything suitable for re-sale, these fairs are very similar to each other today, but they had different origins.

Brough Hill was once described as the largest fair in the North of England and dates back to a charter granted to Robert, Lord Clifford in 1330. It was always held in the autumn so that stock from the fells could be sold before the onslaught of winter. Situated on the higher ground towards Carlisle, this fair in the past attracted dealers from Yorkshire with horses and Scottish dealers with their highland cattle. Game pies of mammoth proportions were provided for the hungry travellers by inn landlords on the route. Stalls were erected by the womenfolk on the roadsides selling all manner of goods to the people passing on their way to the fair. The Yorkshire industrialists from the West Riding woollen mills came to purchase their van horses and the coal mine owners attended to buy their pit ponies.

During the last war the War Office requisitioned the land around and including Brough Hill, so the area allowed for the fair was made a lot smaller.

Appleby Fair celebrated its three hundredth anniversary in June 1985 having existed since 1685 under the protection of a charter granted by James II. For some reason the title was altered about 1750 to the New Appleby Fair and the date moved on a week to its present one. The only reason that comes to mind is that the Gregorian calendar was brought in during 1752 when all dates were altered.

Originally the horse trade was done on the Sands, a stretch of ground between the river Eden and the main road in the town, but later it was moved to Gallows Hill where it is today. In 1911 Gallows Hill was enclosed, having been included in the parish about thirty years earlier. Today the bypass roads fly high above offering the speeding motorist an aerial view of the fair.

The second Tuesday and Wednesday of June are the main fair days but people, horses and caravans start to arrive in the area a few days prior to this. In days gone by the horse-drawn vehicles lined the highways and byeways for

TOP TIPPER TRIO

A Video feature which gives an interesting insight into the typical working environment of three of the country's top tipper trucks.

Running time approx 53 Minutes

C.P.Productions hope you have enjoyed this video programme.
Coming soon - TRUCKING KIWI STYLE featuring British, European & American powered multi-wheel outfits on the highways and byways of New Zealand.

Other titles currently available include:

TRUCK SCENES-ONE - A visual magazine featuring diverse trucking activity in Great Britain, USA, Canada, Sweden, Australia & New Zealand including fridge and tipper operations, complete vehicle bulk woodchip discharging, run-through weighscale stations and the sight and sounds of general & timber haulage in New Zealand.

GREAT LAKES SPECIALS - Focuses on the activities of the unique 11-axle multi-wheel outfits in northern Michigan State, USA including the impressive eight-axle trailer outfits of Cadillac Asphalte and B-Train 'break doubles' hauling coiled steel for the motor industry powered by LTL Fords and other famous North American truck marques.

TRUCKING SWEDISH STYLE - Volvo and Scania trucks engaged in Swedish trucking operations as diverse as timber haulage, milk collections, wood chip haulage, tipper work and quarry work with outsize articulated dump trailers.

ANGELS PLAYMATE - A working day spent on Vancouver Island, Canada with Steve Drybrough and the sight and sounds of his unique 1975 V8 CAT powered Hayes HDX logging truck ascending & descending the summit high in the clouds and conveying loads of up to 200tons to lake discharge at sea level.

WEST COAST EXPERIENCE - Features trucks at work in Oregon & Washington State engaged in transfer/dump operations, truck logging and bulk food products tank operations.

Further features are in the course of production on trucking activities both here in Great Britain and elsewhere around the World.

CPP Videos are distributed exclusively by NYNEHEAD BOOKS

TOP TIPPER TRIO follows three of the country's most exciting trucks as they complete their daily runs. Featured are the unique Maguire Volvo F16 Ambassador; the unusual Scammell/Multidrive outfit belonging to Don Bush and a smart Foden eight wheeler in the livery of Brian Meader and powered by the new Perkins 375. Three of the best indeed!

A CPP Video distributed by Roundoak Publishing, Nynehead, Wellington, Somerset. England TA21 0BX.
£14.99

Beside the River Eden at Appleby on Fair day, c.1920's.

many miles round Appleby and their camp fires and evening sing songs brightened up the night air.

Being the largest assembly of Gypsy and travelling people in Britain there could be about five thousand people in the thiry-acre Fair Hill site all intent on having a good time and doing much business. It must be said that not all visitors to Appleby are true Romanies. Mine workers, general dealers and itinerant workers all attend for the fair's duration.

Always there is the desire in some quarters to close the fair down. The behaviour of a small minority offends the locals and each year some businesses do not open their doors for fear of damage.

Almost single-handed in 1965 Mr. Gordon Boswell, representing the Gypsy people, led and spoke for a deputation that saved this historic meeting place when it was seriously threatened with closure. The locals through their various councils had tried to put an end to the fair and its supporters in the course of their research could not locate the original charter. One document granted by James II dated 31st July 1685 was from the correct period but this seemed to be local to the town of Appleby and did not relate to any horse trading either in or out of the town. It was always thought that all dealings were on Gallows Hill which is just outside the town boundary, so there may be a doubt as to whether this charter actually relates to this fair. There is mention, however, of another fair known as 'New Fair' started in 1750 and given the mayoral seal of approval but no charter could be found for this either.

Most of the painstaking research was done by Viscountess Lowther supported on the County Council by the Honourable Anthony Lowther, M.B.E. This family worked very hard for the Gypsy people and put the case for

Group in front of a bender tent on Fair Hill, Appleby, c.1920's

Far left Mr. Bob Farrow ex-owner of the caravan now in The Castle Museum, York, second left Mr. Shepherdson of Malton. Completing a deal with the traditional handslap at Appleby Horse Fair, c.1930's.

A horse showing off his paces on Fair Hill, Appleby in Westmoreland, c.1950's.

the continuation of the fair at all council meetings. The Member of Parliament for Westmorland at this time was Mr. Michael Jopling and he was taken by the opposers of the fair on a visit round all the worst aspects of the site in 1965. All the bad, dirty areas were shown to him during his two-hour visit and he became convinced that the squalor and filth that he had been directed to was typical of all Romany people. In fact he said so at an impromptu press meeting outside the Shire Hall in Appleby.

At very short notice Mr. Gordon Boswell was asked to speak to the parish council and he put forward his suggestions for a better, more organised fair. He did this magnificently and everyone at the meeting was impressed with his determination, respect and honesty. He also arranged for a collection of well over £100 from the travellers to pay for tidying all the litter from the site after they had left the area. The money was lodged with the Catholic priest Father Caton, who was to hand it over in payment to the agreed contractor after the area was left tidy.

Thankfully at a further meeting, with the Mayor of Appleby's approval and the support of the chairman of the Health and Highways Committee, it was agreed that the fair should continue. Many such meetings, and hours of talking, resulted in the thirty-odd acres of Gallows Hill being made available. The Council would provide water points and latrines and each traveller would pay a fee of £2 to an Appleby Fair fund which would be paid to the Council in return for their facilities.

One of the concessions made by the Gypsies was that the running and trading of horses in the town centre should be stopped and moved to Fair Hill. Sandside next to the river bridge is still the washing point for horses and many younger travellers can be seen with a bottle of washing-up liquid to give their charges a wash and brush up prior to sale.

To supply the demand for china and glassware, salesmen attend Fair Hill and erect flimsy trestle tables to display thousands of pounds worth of Royal Crown Derby and Waterford cut glass. Have a peep into any living trailer, modern or horse-drawn, and you will see displayed this beautiful china and glassware. Waterford, being the best cut glass, is an obvious choice but the presence of Royal Crown Derby is not so easily explained. According to one Romany family, in their early married life fifty or so years ago, this china used to be cheap to buy. Always bright and colourful, the Japan Amari patterns in the rich blues, reds and golds are by far the most popular. From being cheap to collect all those years ago a small bowl now costs about £500 in the better-class gift shops. Travellers still call direct at the factory shop in Osmaston Road, Derby, to make their purchases as well as buying at the fair.

A few details of this special Gypsy collectable china may not be amiss here. Being a fine bone china, Royal Crown Derby traces its ancestry back to the middle years of the 18th century, which was the golden age of the English porcelain manufacturer. A porcelain factory existed in Derby in 1750 but it was in 1765 that William Duesbury set out to create china of unrivalled beauty and excellence. Later he bought the famous Chelsea and Bow factories and transferred the best of their artists and craftsmen to Derby. Here the name Derby china originated.

(Above) The Harker and
Farrow families enjoying a
get-together at Appleby Fair
in the 1950's. Note the large
communal dining tent behind
the caravans.

(Left) Early family group on
Fair day showing the superb
carving and decorative
details on their mobile home.

(Left) Nice shaped bow-top caravan alongside a partly completed square bow near the remains of a camp fire on the Hill at Appleby.

(Below) Washing off the horses in the River Eden at Appleby prior to offering for sale.

Public interest in the various stalls and vehicles for sale on Fair Hill at Appleby.

George III granted William Duesbury the distinction of his patronage and the right to make his china with a crown. In 1890 Queen Victoria commanded that the exquisite ware she had admired should henceforth be marked 'Royal Crown Derby' and this is the unique title proudly used today. The latest honour for this company came in 1978 when they were granted the Royal Warrant by Her Majesty Queen Elizabeth the Queen Mother.

As well as the above-mentioned china and glassware the stalls on the Fair Hill contain harness, pottery and knick-knacks of all descriptions. There is a firm specialising in the buying and selling of gold in all its forms. A pair of scales is on show alongside the day's price of gold and a list of the different hallmarks for all to see.

Gypsy women make and sell children's dresses and cushions made from the brightest of flowered materials.

Fortune tellers abound and today the majority of them are working from very expensive modern trailers complete with lots of chrome and cut glass windows, all offering the best and most accurate readings to their intended clients.

The fair field and adjacent roads and lanes hum with activity. Horses are trotted at a furious pace back and forth along the tarmac with all the skill needed to show off their finer points. Selling of these animals depends on their visual showing during these demonstrations.

There are a few side events like the entertainer who insists on swallowing about fifty feet of 2″ link chain which is trailed through the dust and grime en route to his mouth. He strips to the waist and soon a large gathering forms a circle around him where he works the crowd up into a state of great expectation. Eventually he swallows the chain and his tummy extends, whilst at this point some of the audience feel faint and walk away. Those who continue to watch are asked for a donation from his helpers who mingle with the crowd.

(Top) A deal is sealed with the traditional handshake below the café sign at Appleby Fair in 1985.

(Bottom) Horses waiting to be shod by the blacksmith at Appleby on Fair Hill.

53

As a finale he obtains two or three old beer or milk bottles from the hedgerows and proceeds to break them up on an old plastic sack with a large hammer. When satisfied that the pieces of glass are to his liking he eats them!

Appleby Fair is not all showmanship for the visitor, as most people keep themselves to themselves, sitting around camp fires or just relaxing in the sunshine with occasional journeys into Appleby for provisions or journeys to the public houses. There are always travellers' lorries en route to or from the Hill where anyone who needs a lift just jumps on or clings to the side whilst the vehicle is in motion.

The police are everywhere, usually in pairs, but normally exchange friendly banter with the high-spirited Gypsies as they leave the taverns after closing time. Only when real trouble, fighting or law-breaking occurs do they step in and sort things out. Frequently a fight between travellers will be left to burn itself out as they are usually relations, the fight caused by a boastful incident due to excess alcohol.

If conducted in the spirit of Appleby, all fairs would remain and it is only a handful of thoughtless people who spoil things for the majority. Mr. Gordon Boswell and his fellow travellers worked hard in 1965 to keep this fair alive and it is up to the rest of us to see that it continues as a happy, exciting meeting place in June each year for ever.

Assembling for the 300th anniversary parade at the River Eden bridge in Appleby Town Centre in 1985.

APPLEBY FAIR

by Ron Finch

Thousands of eyes have witnessed,
The beauty of Appleby Fair,
And the gipsys will keep it forever,
Locked and sealed in their care.
It should never be missed by a horseman,
For the best in the world are there,
And you could never forget the beauty,
You saw at Appleby Fair.
Horses in their hundreds of every breed and type,
And the pride of every gypsy is a beautiful black and white.
The cobs are yoked in harness and traces,
And in Bradford carts put through their paces,
With the crack of a whip, a shout and a cry,
Only at Appleby do you see horses fly
With flashing manes and sweeping tails,
They pound the hill on the Cumbrian plains.
Crowds gather on the old stone bridge
With interest they will stare
As the horses in the River are washed with loving care
A sight that can only be seen at the famous Appleby Fair.
The hill is where the gypsies camp every year in June,
Flames flicker gently in the night to the magic of an old gypsy tune,
Stalls are set around the camp and the travellers sell their ware,
China, brass, copper and glass of quality fine and rare.
Horse drawn bow tops, flat carts and open lots have travelled wide and far,
Painted in red, yellow and green these fine paintings must be seen.
Appleby Fair will always be there
The gypsies will keep it forever
Locked and sealed in their care.

55

CHAPTER FOUR

TYPES OF CARAVAN

The Reading Waggon
The Ledge Waggon
The Burton Waggon
The Bow Top
The Open Lot
The Brush Wagon

The first Gypsy caravan most likely originated in India four centuries ago, made from acacia wood, and very heavy but long lasting all the same. The front end was a rectangular box and the back of the car was open with side panels. These sides along with the sides of the box area were ornately decorated with bronze plates fixed to the wood, making it even heavier.

Like the Gypsy caravan known in Yorkshire today this original vehicle was also the family home and contained all the belongings and items used daily. In the box at the front personal belongings were kept rather like we do today in a safe. This would be locked and the valuables safeguarded. In the open middle section sacks of foodstuff and the tools of the trade might be stored — either blacksmith, tinsmith or leatherworker's tools — all items needed to make a living as the family moved about. For nomadic families the caravan held great cultural importance as well as providing shelter and transport.

By the time of the Industrial Revolution roads were improving and from the early to middle nineteenth century the horse-drawn Gypsy caravan started to develop. The style and design was taken from farm vehicles, railway carriages and others but with the originality of the Gypsy incorporated.

The following is a general descripton covering all six main styles.

The Gypsy caravan is a one-roomed living area on four wheels pulled by a horse, and with a door at the front and windows at the back and sometimes also at the sides. It has a cupboard (called a pan box) for pans and food set under the floorboards at the rear where the fresh provisions are kept to be out of the heat of the sun. Steps are set to the front door when the horse is not in the shafts and placed in a rack at the back of the waggon when not needed.

As you look in from the front door there is usually a small cupboard immediately in the left-hand corner with a coal stove just past it on the same side with its chimney protruding out of the roof. Across the far end of the caravan is the bed area in the form of a movable shelf at waist height that can be pulled out to make a double-sized bunk. Halfway along the right-hand side is a table with drawers and finally in the right-hand corner a glass-fronted display unit for crockery and glass. Between all these items of furniture and linking them on both sides are seats, sometimes with lockers underneath them for storage of linen and other household items. Depending on the type of vehicle, and more details will be given about each style later, there may be a window at each side of the caravan, another at the end, and mollicroft roof lights.

Whilst the Romany very rarely made his own caravan from new, as they were manufactured by specialist firms, he had a say in the design and in his personal needs. Much money could be spent on the carvings and gold leaf work and the Gypsy was always very proud of all the finished 'flash.' As the money houses and the building societies never offered loans to travellers whose caravan may have been damaged past all repair and in need of replacement, because it was not classed as a home, all funding had to come out of their own pockets. Whilst not every family could afford to purchase a custom-built caravan, by the 1950's many had turned to living in the modern motor-pulled trailer, the pulling vehicle being used during the day for the general business of collecting scrap metal or whatever.

Today in the 1980's a small number still live in horse-drawn units, but tend to be either very poor, unable to afford any other, or the more adventurous younger travellers who wish to return to the old ways.

Developing from the bender tent and the rough simple accommodations fixed to carts, the following main styles of caravan have emerged.

The Reading Waggon

The Reading waggon was the most beautiful of the Romany caravans named after the area where it was first made. Never seen as much in Yorkshire as in the South of England its style and shape were copied by other makers.

It was built to about eleven feet in body length with an additional fourteen to eighteen inches (depending where the measurement is taken from) for a front and rear porch. The width of the bed area was six feet six inches across the rear of the waggon.

Due to the design of large wheels at the rear and smaller ones at the front, the caravan had a ground clearance of just over four feet and made it most suitable for the rougher and rutted country roads of the time. The back wheel diameter was sixty inches and the front wheel diameter forty-two inches. The overall weight of the finished caravan would be about one and a half tons, so a good strong horse or horses were required to pull it.

Timber used in its construction varied from one area to the next but in the main pine was used for the frame of the body as it was a good straight grained timber. Oak, being very heavy, was used only where the area of the waggon would get a lot of wear and knocks. Ash, sycamore and mahogany were used in carved areas for strength and toughness. The bodywork was match-boarded to the penny farthing style, so called because the width of the wood was the same as the width of the old penny and the farthing when placed side by side. These boards were supported on the outside by chamfered uprights, the patterns of which were carved with a draw knife or sometimes just a penknife. These chamfers were both decorative when painted and weight reducing, whilst retaining their original purpose of supporting the matchboard sides.

(Top) One of the last fully preserved Reading vans in use at Fairs today prior to being very badly damaged in a road accident in 1985, but now fully restored again to its former glory.

(Bottom) Mr. Tom Harrison with the Hood family on the steps of the Hood's ornate Reading caravan at Gilling, North Yorkshire, in the 1950's. This vehicle was sold at this time for £75.

The later Reading vans had a mollicroft set of roof windows added for extra light. This was favoured by the showpeople who spent more of their time inside than the Gypsy whose time was spent in the open air. When the Showmen's Guild was formed at the start of this century one criteria for being able to join was that the living waggon had mollicroft windows; the reason being that whilst the Guild did not wish to differentiate between classes of people they only wanted the wealthier ones to join as members. Hence the richer showmen would all qualify, having the required window in their homes, whereas the poorer showmen and most of the Gypsies would not.

All doors on the Gypsy designed Reading waggons opened outwards while the ones intended for showmen opened inwards. Why this was so is not clear but could have been someone's personal preference that stuck.

There were glass windows in the split half-door and sash windows at each side with a small rear window above the bed area. The side and rear windows may have had louvre shutters that provided air in the summer and masked out the interior light in the winter. It must be remembered that when the Gypsy was travelling and parked in a quiet lane he wanted to remain undetected by officials so that he would not be moved on; a light in his window at night was not to his advantage. Sometimes, and especially if there was a bow-shaped window in an open-lot, coloured glass in blues and reds may have been incorporated in the design, giving an internal warmth of light.

The louvre shutters slotted into a waist board that ran just below the window area and formed a channel for the window to fit and slide. This board was carved and decorated and made into a feature.

Being so high off the ground and to save constant standing on the shafts when entering or leaving the interior, the Reading was sometimes fitted with an iron step. On all other types of caravan this feature was not normally needed as they were nearer the ground.

The roof may have been made of felt (bitumin) or canvas over timber boards running the water into a gutter at each side with a natural fall to each end of the waggon, terminating in an open-mouthed lion's head gargoyle to let the water out. The weatherboards surrounding these gutters were usually chamfered and decorated. At each side of the front and rear porches were the most elaborate carved bracket supports containing three dimensional designs of leaves, flowers and twigs, all intertwined.

Duntons of Reading were the main builders of these waggons, if not the actual instigator of them, from the 1880's till the firm was sold in 1922. The only drawings that were made were on the back of cigarette packets or rough scraps of paper and later lost or destroyed. Each vehicle took six months to a year to complete and some are now in safe keeping in museums dotted around the country.

The Ledge Waggon

The Ledge, or cottage-loaf shaped waggon, was so named due to its similarity to the household bread loaf. A narrow base widens out from about sixteen inches above the floorboards to make a Reading waggon width. This extension goes out over the wheels and is supported by 'swan neck' brass scroll supports.

Not as ornately carved as the Reading, the matchbord sides are usually cut off in the porch areas to make a curved shape and are themselves carved and gilded at the ends to make a decorative pattern. Whereas the Reading matchboarding continues all the way down the sides, the area below the ledge on this waggon may be mahogany panel with rib surrounds. This gave scope for either carving or decorative scrollwork.

At the front end under the ledge may be constructed chicken or bantam coups from turned spindles. A spindle door could be opened for the entry or removal of the fowls.

The Ledge waggon was made in most parts of Britain and was a more popular vehicle with showmen than the Romany.

The Burton Waggon

As the name suggests the waggon was not actually made in Yorkshire but at Burton-upon-Trent by a firm called Orton, Sons & Spooner. As they were mainly builders of the very ornate fairground rides and bioscopes of the latter part of the last century, they tended to supply the needs of fairground people more than the Gypsies. This type was made elsewhere by Duntons of Reading and Hawcrofts of Hartlepool but not in any quantity.

The showmen usually stayed on the better roads and liked the larger size of

Burton waggon owned and restored by Mr. Paul B. Benn from Frimley Green, Surrey, showing the simple but practical design favoured mainly by the showmen and circus people.

(Top) Mr. A. Alexander's Showman's van prior to its restoration in Malton and its return to Halifax in the West Riding of Yorkshire.

(Bottom) The same vehicle fully restored in rich maroon and yellow underworks with off-white trim.

61

interior because of its straight-sided design and added mollicroft roof lights. Not needing to be on rough ground like the Gypsy sometimes found himself, the traveller did not find the heavier vehicle a disadvantage. Burton waggons varied from the small, and to some extent plainer, to the very ornate large ones. One specially built for the Murphy family early this century was 30ft. long and weighed 10 tons, containing every stylish addition like panelled mahogany, electric light, fire and radiators. It cost about £3,500. The smaller ones may have cost about £200 complete.

The Burton waggon was constructed with panels or matchboard like the Reading waggon and also had the mollicroft roof for better internal light; sometimes it was very plain, but at other times, it had ornate carved oak porch brackets in keeping with the fairground style of decoration.

The Bow-Top

The bow-top is the caravan style most favoured by the Gypsy. Even so it was always more popular in the North of England than the South. Its ten foot length and light weight may have been its main attraction. Due to the top being canvas over a bent ash wood frame it does not have anything like the weight of the previously mentioned caravans. As it does not have the mollicroft windows or the side timbers of the others its total weight is in the region of one ton whereas the Reading and the Ledge would be about one and a half tons.

The bows were steam bent ash $2\frac{1}{2}''$ wide by $\frac{3}{4}''$ thick spaced between twelve and sixteen inches apart and covered with insulation material and waterproof canvas. The insulation material could be old fashioned carpet underfelt or sometimes carpet itself with the pattern downwards to be seen as decoration from inside the waggon.

Shapes of bows varied a little with different manufacturers from round barrel top to the more depressed horseshoe shape and the flatter barrel top favoured by the Swinefleet makers. Occasionally, and a rarity these days, a square shaped bow top would be made. Unlike the round ones, this model may have windows set in the canvas sides which allows more light into the interior.

The bow top had a ledge which formed an internal seat. To protect the canvas from the backs of those seated, matchboarding was fitted on the inside up to about shoulder height. Sometimes the space under the ledge or seat inside the waggon was filled in with lockers which made a very useful addition to the limited storage.

The bow top had large wheels at the rear and smaller ones at the front and could, like the Reading, travel on fairly uneven ground and still keep upright.

The Open-Lot

The open-lot waggon became popular between the two Great Wars and is still built today by the traveller who wishes to take to the road as cheaply as possible.

The most simple of all the caravans for the semi-skilled to make for himself, it fits neatly on to an existing four-wheeled flat cart. The turntable, springs and floorboards are all there just to build the top onto. Internally the layout resembles other Gypsy caravans with a stove just inside the door on the left

A Bill Wright Bow-top pictured after completion in their yard at Rothwell Haig, Leeds, c.1906. The chicken coup can be seen under the ledges at the front on each side of the waggon.

about three bow spaces down, and seating on either side. A table and cupboard are situated halfway down on the right-hand side and the bed lies across the rear of the waggon. Spanning the caravan at its broadest point the bed with its deceptive six foot three inch width when pulled out into its night-time position forms an ample double bed.

The rear view of a large Wright's bow-top outside the Malt Shovel Inn, Hovingham, North Yorkshire. The louvre shutters can be drawn over the windows at night time by running in the two channels at top and bottom. The square 'pan box' under the floorboards is actually the food larder, as it is the coolest place on the waggon.

The same caravan prior to its fire and stove pipe being added.

At the back end would be a small oblong window and louvre shutters or occasionally, like the bow-top, a small bow window with stained glass inserts in leaded lights.

There are no doors at the front of this style; hence the name of 'open-lot.' A canvas sheet forms protection during the daytime from the cold and rain. At night a curtain might be suspended from hoops under the porch and dropped down to fill the front area.

Positioned with its back into the bad weather and containing a small 'Queenie' stove, this is a very cosy little unit and one much favoured by the Northern travellers for its easy handling and comparative cheapness to make.

The Brush Waggon

Finally in this section we must mention the brush waggon. Whilst not really a Gypsy caravan it must rank as one of the most ornate vehicles of its time. It was used mainly by travelling salesmen to display and sell their goods as they travelled the country. Household items including cane chairs, brooms, mops and oilcloths were all displayed in the side lockers and on the roof racks.

This was the home as well as the shop for the salesman and his family. The most unique features of this horse-drawn showroom are the rear door and fixed steps. Unlike the previously mentioned caravans, whose doors were at the front end, it could be that in the case of the brush waggon the horse was always in the shafts when the shop was open and it would be far easier for prospective customers to gain entry from the rear unimpeded.

Only two of these vehicles have survived to this day and both are in private ownership in the South of England. However the pre-1910 photograph taken in Wheelgate, Malton, Yorkshire, does show their existence here in the North also.

Bow-top at Chestnut Farm, Acaster Malbis, York. The stained glass rear window is a nice feature as well as its butterfly chamfers on the inside of the wheel felloes.

Nice wide Open-lot with interesting scrollwork, parked up in the 1950's.

Superbly restored Open-lot at Mr. Robert Farrow's, Canal Head, Pocklington, East Yorkshire, in 1985. Perfect bow shape and good internal height for standing. The grape motif on the rear window is etched on to the glass.

A rear view of the same caravan.

The interior of a miniature Open-lot owned and kindly set out by Mrs. Betty Farrow of Kirkbymoorside, North Yorkshire, with Crown Derby china and waterjack.

(Top) Rare example of a Brush waggon pictured in Wheelgate, Malton, North Yorkshire, c.1910. Note the rear entry steps and the items of furniture on top and sides.

(Bottom) 1 Example of a bender tent in use at Appleby Fair 1984 with Ainlee Ryalla and Verity posing in the entrance.

CHAPTER FIVE

MAKERS OF CARAVANS

Throughout Yorkshire there were many small builders of carts and caravans. Most towns and villages had their joiner, wheelwright and blacksmith who worked together to produce vehicles for the farms and hauliers. One or two of these craftsmen branched out into other forms of horse-drawn transport and the best known of these for building the Gypsy caravans were William Wright of Rothwell Haigh, Leeds, Fred Hill of Swinefleet near Goole, Uriah Hurst and his two sons of Woodlesford near Leeds and R. W. Hodgson of Halifax.

All these firms did general waggon and cart building but specialised in the Gypsy living vehicles as part of their business.

William Wright

William Wright was born in 1844, and died on the 20th November 1909 aged 65 years. He is buried in the village churchyard of Rothwell where his grave is marked by a granite cross.

He founded his firm of waggon builders when only twenty-one years old in 1865, and this is proudly printed on his letterhead. His two sons, Herbert

The Wright Brothers in their yard at Rothwell Haig, Leeds, with a newly completed general dealer's vehicle, c.1906.

(Right) Mr. William Wright and dog posing in front of a nearly completed Bow-top waggon, c.1906.

(Bottom) Newly completed Ledge waggon leaving Messrs. Wright Brothers' yard at Rothwell Haig, near Leeds, c.1906.

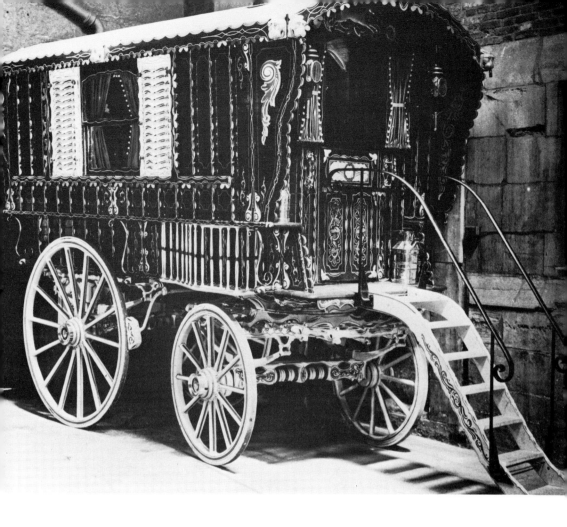

(Top) A perfect example of a Bill Wright waggon fully restored by the Romany decorator Mr. Jimmy Berry at the Castle Museum, York, in the early 1960's.

(Bottom) William Wright billhead copy.

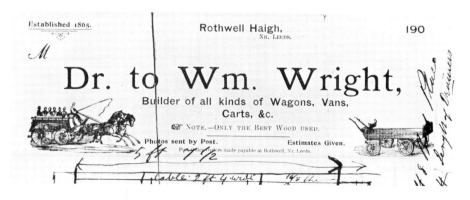

and Albert, both joined him in the business, the former specialising in the joinery side and the latter in blacksmithing and painting. Many caravans like the ones illustrated were produced at their works over a period of sixty years, the last being built in 1926. However, the firm continued until the death of Albert in 1932 and Herbert in 1952, when the workshop area was sold for building purposes.

In a manufacturing process of this complexity many outside suppliers of parts were required and the list available at The Castle Museum, York, of the Wrights' main suppliers is in itself a most interesting document. All the larger firms they had dealings with were listed in a day book along with the items most usually supplied, in some cases with their prices.

For example it is written that W. Harker & Son of Leeds provided spokes, and in March 1911 there is an entry that 50 spokes $17\frac{1}{2}''$ and $18\frac{1}{2}''$ long cost £1 0s. 10d; and that Messrs. Asquiths supplied a pair of hoops for the wheels size 3' 2" x 2" x $\frac{3}{4}''$ for 15/9d. Messrs. Norman Smee and Didwell of London were the varnish makers as were Messrs. Noble & Honi of London. J. Denison of Doncaster provided the ingredients for paint making (as all paint was mixed on the premises and not ready-made as today) — orange lead, white lead, boiled linseed oil, American turps and goldsize. Messrs. William Nicholson & Son of Leeds supplied best pine matching timber of a size 3" x $\frac{1}{2}''$ for the sum of one old penny per running foot. Birch board, naves and blocks came from J. M. Hutchinson (Timber Merchants), Leeds. Nave covers (German Silver), stays, shaft ends, tugs, stays for seats, hoops for back of naves were supplied by Messrs. J. Hindle (Brass Founder), Leeds. Most of the ironwork, e.g. springs, was obtained from Jonas Woodhead and Sons, Leeds.

The most interesting entry found in the day book was the name and address hand written inside the back cover of a Mr. H. F. Kirk, 4a Fox & Grape Yard, Kirkgate, Leeds, with the single entry 'woodcarver.' It is well known that William Wright's vehicles had the timber rough shaped and positioned in place before being numbered on the back and sent off to an outside carver craftsman. Could Mr. Kirk be responsible for the beautiful grapes and leaves and jumping horses featured on the caravans that came out of the yard at Rothwell Haigh?

Gypsies visited this busy yard and watched closely their orders being completed. The builder, always wary not to be caught out over the final payment, and partly because the doors of the workshop were not high enough, built the entire caravan on a low bogey. When finished and the final payment made the contraption was pushed out of the workshop into the yard, where the wheels were fitted. The vehicle was now ready for the road, or almost, as it is said that the final touch was to dust the grape carvings with chalk to give them that natural 'bloom' finish.

While Herbert and Albert were craftsmen in their own right father William was something of an inventor. What line of thought or research prompted him to take a patent out for a closet (toilet) ventilator may never be known, but he did. This consisted of a hole in the ceramic toilet pan above the water level, with a hollow pottery pan leading to a vent at the back that joined a stove pipe through the closet roof, topped off with a cowl. Perhaps the idea just came to him as he sat and pondered about the infection caused by the smells and germs not being able to readily escape. The total cost of this Leeds Fireclay closet with natural whitewood seat, pipe, regulator and cowl was £2 18s. 0d, but, sadly, it was never a great success.

Uriah Hurst

Uriah Hurst was Wright's foreman. He went into partnership with his two sons at Woodlesford and they traded as Hurst Brothers producing caravans in the same shape and style as Wrights. So near were the designs and colours and so good was the workmanship that they are often mistaken for the Rothwell Haigh waggons.

R. W. Hodgson of Halifax only built a few caravans in the style and shape of Wright before he went out of business.

Fred Hill

Fred Hill started in 1894 in Swinefleet after an apprenticeship in Alford and from a starting capital of about £50 he went on to create with his son one of the (if not the) largest wheelwright and builders' firms in Yorkshire. At the height of their business eleven men were fully employed.

The first caravan was built in 1899 for a travelling showman just five years after the firm started. It was another eight years before the first Gypsy caravan was produced. Once this caravan was seen by other Gypsies and the word spread their fame was assured and a continual stream of callers to the Swinefleet works provided work for years to come.

Mr. Roland Hill joined his father in 1911 as an apprentice and taught hmself every side of the trade from joinery and wheelwrighting to painting and lettering where required. Even for an expert like Mr. Hill it took two complete weeks to finish the decoration on each caravan and six months working full time to actually make it.

The last Gypsy caravan was made by Hills in 1946 and they eventually went on to produce the modern aluminium-bodied ones known today. In fact they were possibly the first firm to add aluminium bodies to the Model 'T' Ford chassis long before they became popular.

Hills were a very complete firm as they could cope with all the trades needed to produce vehicles on their large site. As they expanded, their works covered a two-acre site. They had workshops for making the waggons, a metal forge, a paintshop, a sawmill, a lathe shop, a blacksmith's shop, and so could manufacture a Gypsy caravan almost from start to finish.

Fred Hill died in 1946 and his eldest son Roland continued the business until his mother died in 1964 when he himself retired.

The Wheelwright

The wheelwright was an essential craftsman in the making of a Gypsy caravan. Many villages fifty years ago would have their own wright who would serve the needs of the surrounding area, and most of the cart and caravan makers had their own workshop.

The skill in making a complete wheel started with the selection and buying of the standing timber. Ash, oak, elm and beech were the ones most frequently used and all these had different properties when seasoned. It was always preferable to fell the oak tree when the sap had started to rise in spring as this dried and added strength to the wood's structure.

Oak was better for cleaving (chopping) into spokes as the length of the timber's grain gave extra strength and a spoke if cut on a band saw may have a cross grain that could snap when in position in the finished wheel.

Sometimes the trees had already been felled when inspected by the wheelwright and the bark removed for the tanning industry. From these butts, or logs, he would select what was required to be moved into his premises to be cut, stacked and seasoned. It was not so important when the other timbers were felled but they had not to be left standing on the damp earth in the round for a long time as they would rot internally because of the moisture trapped inside. More important, and this is where local knowledge came in, the wright had to know which areas and soil conditions produced the best quality timbers.

When buying standing timber a special marker knife, very similar to the type for releasing stones from horses' hooves, was used to cut a mark in the bark that would be recognised by the person collecting it. Nowadays anyone buying timber in this form uses a can of spray dye that marks the tree.

After the butts had stood in the yard for a week or two to dry and settle, a team of specialist sawyers arrived to cut them into planks. Most yards had a pit, similar to a garage inspection pit, where a man positioned himself in the bottom holding one end of the long two-man saw while his mate was up at ground level controlling the speed and thickness of the operation. As the logs were rolled lengthways over the hole the slow process of the hand sawing would eventually be completed. Nothing is more exciting than looking at the new cut face of the timber and seeing if the grain is straight and good for the purpose for which it was purchased. All the tree butts were inspected before sawing took place and the lengths and thicknesses were all decided in advance of cutting so that there was little waste. The different uses that the timber was going to be put to determined how it was cut at this stage. Then the pieces of planked wood were stacked in a corner of the yard, preferably in the shade, with slivers of wood between each section to allow the free passage of air to dry out the sap. If stacked in the direct heat of the sun cracking could occur and ruin the planks. Gradual drying in the breeze was best.

A year was estimated to be the usual time to leave the stacks for each 1″ of timber thickness. They would be then cut into the required shapes for the jobs they were intended for. Felloe blocks of ash would be rough cut and placed in stacks to allow the air to circulate again, but this would be inside the building and not outside as no rain had to dampen the stacks at this stage. Likewise the elm blocks were cut for the hubs and great care had to be taken in the seasoning of these as a resin powder formed which had to be dusted off every few weeks for the first year to prevent the timber rotting. After seven to ten years these could be considered fully seasoned and dry and could be selected for the wheel hubs. The long delay from buying to using the timber meant a lot of money was laid out in stock but there was no quicker way if the best quality end product was required.

Mr. Richard Gill and family, carriage builders and restorers, Brame Lane, Norwood, Harrogate, North Yorkshire, fixing metal channel tyre to wooden wheel.

Once the timber had been selected and roughed out to season, the wheel could be made. For a Gypsy caravan the wheel size was from 34″ to 38″ diameter for the smaller ones and up to 60″ for the larger one on the Reading type waggons. The elm hub would be morticed out by hand originally, but by machine in more modern times. This is where the co-ordination of the hand and the eye and the experience of the craftsman came into play. He would know exactly where to cut and at what depth of angle for the spokes to make a perfect job. Spokes were clefted; the end fitting the morticed joint of the hub was square and the end fitting into the felloes was rounded so that it would not twist with use. Two spokes to each felloe were neatly pegged and tightened from the outside edge prior to fitting the iron tyre. The assembled wheel, put together as tightly as the wheelwright could with the use of spoke jacks and clamps, was eventually screwed down tight onto a large flat iron disc outside in the yard area. The iron tyre having been measured round the wheel felloes with a 'traveller' and the required length of straight iron cut off to the size needed, the ends were bent in a tyre bending machine and then fired to heat and join them on the anvil.

The completed round iron tyre was then put in a timber fire until red hot and when ready placed over the tightened wood felloes until it started to smoke but not actually fire. This burning caused the ironwork to seat itself onto the wood for a good fit. After a few seconds the wheelwright and his assistants had to

Jarvis Browning, the farrier from Normanby, North Yorkshire, at work shoeing a horse at the Ryedale Folk Museum, Hutton-le-Hole.

pour cold water round the rim from all sides at the same time so that the cooling contracted the iron which in turn tightened all the wood joints of the wheel. The felloes tightened to the spokes which in turn tightened to the nave or hub and at this stage it was known if a good wheel had been made. One that was too slack would not last and one that was too tight would split.

The Blacksmith and Farrier

In describing the various processes in the manufacture of caravans we must not forget the pulling power — the horse.

Good strong animals were needed to be able to manage the twenty or thirty hundredweights of caravan, and the Gypsy normally favoured the heavy cob-type horse. Training from young by taking out with an older experienced animal was the best way to get horses used to road and traffic. Any old horse from the farms would be unsuitable for pulling a caravan as it would not have the temperament or nature to do so satisfactorily. If used on hilly ground the addition of another horse, or sideliner, was a great advantage and could be fixed to a spreader arm attached to the offside summer support or to the rear of the waggon on the same side. So gentle yet so courageous, these horses were treated with all the love and affection given to a member of the family. While the animal itself obtains most of its health requirements from nature when grazing, as it will instinctively select any herbs it needs, occasionally the

Craftsman saddler making new harness sitting astride his special work-horse.

professional help of the farrier may be called upon. This is a job needing special skill and understanding not always possessed by the Gypsy himself and is most important as a lame animal is no use to anyone.

If the horse is in regular use on hard metal roads, shoeing will need to be done every two hundred miles or so. As a daily journey could be anything from five to twenty miles the time between one shoeing and the next would vary. A very close watch on the horse's legs, the way it walked, and any unusual strains or limps would be keenly noted and the correct treatment given.

CHAPTER SIX

DECORATORS AND RESTORERS

The scroll-shaped decoration with coach lining is a special feature of the Gypsy caravan but the origins of this are little known.

As the caravan itself only evolved in the late 19th century and the early models carried very little painted decoration there has not been much time for patterns to develop, so it can only be conjecture on our part as to its origin. It is generally known that the Gypsy has always enjoyed the bright colours found in nature and it seems understandable that he would wish for these to be transferred to his living waggon. Primrose or jasmine yellow, rich crimson, leaf or grass green, light oak are the colours mainly used in decoration.

The influence of the coach builder and wheelwright showed itself with the general line work on the caravans as most of them were built to the Gypsies' requirements in the workshops of the olden day craftsmen. Scrolls, or curlicue patterns, have long been seen in the artwork of this country and abroad but when, or if, they were copied for caravan decoration is pure speculation.

Mastering the use of the chisel-ended paint brush and the longer lining 'ducks' as well as the application of gold leaf were certainly skills requiring expert knowledge and practice. In Yorkshire there could have been many travellers that decorated their own vehicles very competently but the two greatest craftsmen who were always available to complete work for others were Jimmy Berry and Tommy Gaskin. During the last fifty years these two men have commanded the respect and admiration of generations of travellers and non-travellers alike. It is said that the former taught the latter in his art but one suspects that each would have been able to achieve this without the other's influence in some form or another.

Jimmy Berry was a man who was continually on the move with no set roots, never wishing to stay in one place longer than the job in hand. Stories abound of him being able to complete a perfect scroll with a brush in each hand, or to use the hairs from his horse's tail to make his liners; using blades of grass to apply the broader lines when working out in the open countryside; visiting the public house, after which he was able to work better, and reputed to be able to copy on the waggon the engraved glass pattern of the pub window from memory. Proof of the modesty of this man is that he has never thought of himself as a full-time Gypsy caravan painter and to him the greatest moment was to beat the panel of 'What's My Line?' on television some twenty years ago.

Tommy Gaskin made his home in the Ackworth district of Yorkshire though his birthplace was understood to be South Wales. He was well-known for making and converting bow-top caravans and completing the gold leaf

These photographs show Mr. Jimmy Berry starting to restore the Wrights' Ledge Waggon in the Castle Museum, York, in the early 1960's.

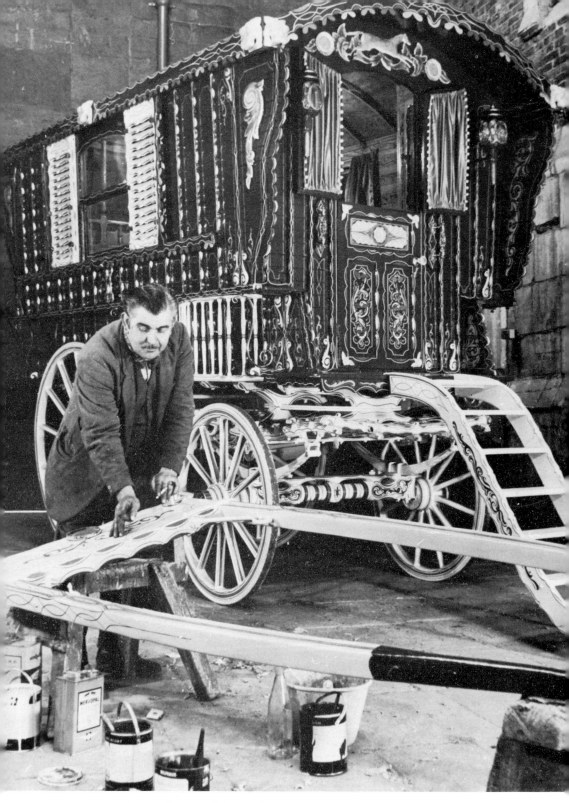

Mr. Jimmy Berry with his work at the Castle Museum nearly completed.

scrollwork and decorations himself. Sometimes he would use his palm as a pallet and with the thumb of his other hand apply the colour to the butterfly chamfers. Many examples of his work can be seen in both private and museum collections. He died in 1984 and received a very good send off from his many friends at one of the largest funerals seen for many a year in his home area.

Occasionally a traveller did complete his own painting but this tended to lack the free flow of the professional decorator. The speed of working depends on the capability of the artist and the quality of the finished work but two or three weeks is about right for a good job on a Gypsy caravan.

At this point two Pickering brothers must really be mentioned. Whilst not strictly caravan painters, Bob and Peter Taylor could, if they set their minds to it, produce a really first class job. Peter can make any wooden part of a flatcart or rulley and understands the mechanics of all the working parts. Bob, on the other hand, decorates the traditional Gypsy flat carts from his workshop in Pickering with all the colour and finish that one expects. Unfortunately he can only paint part-time as he has a business to run but even so the volume of work he has completed over the years and the standard he has attained would have made him a first-class full-time decorator had he so wished.

Percy Hornshaw from Dunnington near York was a very popular restorer, especially of wheels, for the Gypsies. They would call at his 'old world' premises in the village main street having left their caravans just outside on the lay-by until their work was completed.

Mr. Hornshaw was a craftsman, making and restoring many horse-drawn types of vehicles for the large private estates in the area. Tragically the son who would have continued the business was killed in an accident as a young man; the workshop and yard closed on Mr. Hornshaw's passing in the early 1980's.

Two caravans being decorated c.1900 for Annie Holland's fairground bioscope.

The Author putting the finishing touches to the carved grapes on a newly restored Bow-top.

Applying the outline to the scrollwork with a long-haired line brush.

The Author on the left with the owner Mr. John Henderson after the completed restoration of this 1905 Bow-top. In 1978 this caravan was sold in auction to the Abbey House Museum at Leeds for £4,000.

The Author making a start on the restoration of a Showman's vehicle.

CHAPTER SEVEN

RESTORATION TECHNIQUES

The restoration work in this chapter, because it is restoration and not original work, has to be described in modern terms. It is not intended to be a historical narrative, as this has been dealt with elsewhere in more detail, but to assist the modern restorer and owner in his work.

In the days when the Gypsy caravan was in everyday use, the owner did his own repairs and decorations as the need arose.

While the caravan was stationary and the women out calling the men might decide to alter, repair or add to an existing vehicle.

Sun is the main cause of general deterioration and as the wood shrinks and dries the rain will soak in causing rot. On the larger waggons the owners hung a canvas sheet on the side facing the sun to protect it and most caravan owners put wet sacking over the wheels to stop them drying out.

Great care, and a lot of pride, was taken in the upkeep of the family home as this was a talking point at the fairs and gatherings where people met. Also it had a monetary value and often would be 'chopped' or sold unknowingly to the womenfolk either for horses or another caravan.

A newly-wed couple might have been given a small caravan as a wedding present by one or other of the parents and at a later date they would swap or trade it for a larger one to accommodate a possible family.

Due to the age-old tradition of burning the caravan on the owner's death, many hundreds of first-class vehicles have been destroyed for ever. Those that have remained, due to being sold out of Romany ownership or saved by those not sticking so faithfully to the Romany tradition, are the ones being restored and cared for now.

Many people, Gypsies included, may only be able to see an example of a genuine Romany caravan in a museum or possibly in non-Gypsy ownership. Even though some travelling families might have a horse-drawn caravan in their possession, only about ten families in Great Britain actually live in one all the year round. The fairs attract the caravans of those who still have an yen to be out on the open road and even though they may appear on the back of a low-loader only for the fair's duration the family can go back in time to their previous way of life.

Wealthy non-Gypsy people have purchased Romany caravans as some form of status symbol to place beside a swimming pool or just to have as a garden ornament. Whilst this may seem a sad state of affairs at least the caravans themselves have been preserved for future generations to enjoy.

The easiest way to describe a total restoration is to imagine the non-Gypsy reader wishing to purchase a caravan in a sad state of repair and to explain the points to watch out for and the ways of making a complete restoration.

Looking at the drab shell of a horse-darawn caravan, the prospective buyer is faced with a daunting task to bring it up to its former colour and glory. However, do not be put off, but work your way carefully through the vehicle watching out for the following points.

First walk right round the caravan from a distance of about twenty feet, if this is possible and the vehicle is not crowded into a small shed, and get an overall impression of its shape and condition. The shape is important because if there is a major structural fault it will show up in the shape. The Ledge, Reading and Burton types will have nice even sides gently sloping to the eaves, whereas the bow-tops and open-lots should have a straight ridge if viewed from the side as well as a gentle tilt outwards for the porch and rear areas.

It goes without saying that a horse-drawn vehicle must depend upon its wheels. These are wood spoked with an iron tyre holding them together. Take notice if the present owner has taken the trouble to raise all four wheels off the ground onto blocks as this stops any damp and water getting between the iron tyre and the wooden felloe causing rot. Always carry a pen knife, and preferably without the owner watching, as he may take offence, gently prod the outside wood area of the wheel and make sure it is sound. With the handle of the knife or another hard object lightly tap each spoke in turn and listen for the ring sound. If a dull thud is heard, the chances are that the spoke in question could be rotten and need replacing. If not repaired the spoke may snap and cause problems for the wheel at a later date.

Having satisfied yourself that the wheels are in good order have a look at all the wooden ledges and joints where water could settle and cause timbers to rot. Look for any damage to the underworks possibly by being dropped too heavily off a low-loader or lorry in transit. Shafts, pan box, steps, and rack should all be there to make the vehicle complete.

Next inspect the inside. If raining when you call to view look out for damp getting in. If viewed at night time, which you should hardly ever do, look for any outside light showing through cracks or holes in the roof area or sides. Examine the drawers, cupboards, shelves and floor for woodworm or rot; the stove and pipe for safety and condition.

All this has to be observed and inspected in a few moments as you do not always have the time to dally and the vendor is keen to make a sale. If you decide to buy then the task of restoration really begins. Assuming that you are able to work under cover without the fear of rain disturbing your efforts the job is made that bit simpler. First remove all the old wood, canvas, leather and metal that is going to be of no use to you but keep any items on hand for future reference if you need a pattern to copy from.

All types of caravan may be treated in the same way but obviously there will be variations between the Reading and bow-top styles.

The most obvious difference in the restoration required between the Reading, Ledge and Burton waggon and the bow-top will be the roof area. The larger waggons nearly always have a double roof with windows set into the smaller top section called the mollicroft. The general shape over the roof area is

The Ryedale Folk Museum Open-lot prior to its restoration in 1981. The front doors and windows were removed to bring it back to its original style.

formed by wide tongued and grooved boarding usually in pine and covered with bitumen and zinc felt, all water running down to a lead-lined gutter at each side of the caravan with a decorative lion's head gargoyle at each end for it to escape from.

Repairs to this kind of roof will need the knowledge and expertise of a good craftsman joiner and the method of application will be common sense. With the canvas-covered bow-top and open-lot caravan a few little tips may be of use to the first-time restorer. Having taken off the old worn and damaged sheet exposing the ash bows, or framework of the roof area, first check that they are not damaged and that there are no bolts or nails sticking out to puncture the new canvas when it is placed over. Straight over the bows from side to side, you should butt up lengths of the old-fashioned half-inch thick carpet underfelt, never the modern foam rubber kind as the vehicle cannot breathe. By butting the edges together and not overlapping there will be no unsightly join marks when the canvas is tightened over the top.

Have the green weatherproof canvas made a foot larger than actually needed

(Above) Some of the hundreds of metal parts from the underworks of a caravan taken apart to restore. All items were sandblasted prior to painting and re-fitting.

(Left) Bending bows the natural way at the Ryedale Folk Museum, Hutton-le-Hole, North Yorkshire.

Fixing the carpet underfelt insulation and weatherproof sheet over the bows on the 1923 caravan in the Ryedale Folk Musuem, 1981.

at each end of the roof and also at the lower edges. The seams are better if they go over the waggon and not along it, as there will be no pressure on the stitching, but this is personal preference. Whilst at the makers ask them to fix four eyelets equi-distant along the bottom edges so that you can fix weights to these when fitted loose over the waggon. The best weight is an old-fashioned wood ladder tied full length down each side but a long solid log or balk of timber would do just as well. The main thing to watch is that the tension applied is even as this exercise is designed to stretch the fabric fibres for a better, closer fit. Allow the weights to stay on the draped canvas for about two or three days, preferably having rain or dew on it, and when dry remove the weights and start to fix down using large-headed carpet tacks.

From a ladder placed at the end of the caravan roof tack into the side of the end bow in the middle. Place about three or four tacks in a similar position down each side of the same bow from the centre at six inch intervals. Then move the ladder and yourself to the other end of the caravan and after pulling the canvas as tight as you can towards you over the top of the roof area repeat the fixing method just applied to the other end. Only work a yard or so down each side of the centre and then concentrate on fixing to the middle at the base of the sheet. Pull down hard and tack at intervals making sure that the sheet is even and that the joints run straight over the waggon. To help at this stage, and to leave the hands free for hammer and tacks, use the eyelets previously used for hanging the weights and tie strong string to one of these with a loop at foot height from the ground. Placing the foot into this loop enables the canvas to be tightened and tacked into position at the same time.

When the canvas is finally secure with tacks all the way round, cut off the spare canvas with a carpet knife and then fix the decorative woodwork over the tack heads to cover these from view.

The secret of fixing a good canvas to a waggon is that it tightens when wet and slackens when dry but never too much either way or it will split when tight and flap when slack.

After the canvas and underfelt are safely in place the caravan will then be waterproof but you will need to fix your stove and pipe in position for internal warmth and cooking facilities.

The most popular model for the smaller caravans is the 'Queenie' wood and coal burning stove, thought to have originated in the U.S.A. in the 1830's by the founder of the present company that produces it, Messrs. Smith & Wellstood Esse Limited from Scotland. Twenty-three year old James Smith set up business in Jackson, Mississippi, in 1839 and, amongst other things, fitted out the waggons heading west with pots, pans and stoves. Born in Edinburgh on the 4th June 1816 he was the second child (of eleven) of James Smith, a shawl manufacturer and a native of Paisley. When he returned to Scotland to set up the business of Smith & Wellstood in 1854 he brought with him several of the "American pattern stoves," one of which was the Queen.

The No.6 Queen is still in production to date but stoves are also made by at least two other U.K. companies; even in 1885 it was 'pirated' by others.

The stove is always fitted on the left-hand side of the caravan when looking in from the door from the front, between the third and fourth bow. Stand the stove on the caravan floor facing the interior at right angles to the sides and cut a hole slightly larger than the diameter of the stove pipe directly above the stove in the canvas and underfelt. Then from a ladder on the outside drop the full length of pipe through this hole and rest it over the aperture on top of the stove. You will appreciate that the fitting cannot be left like this for reasons of safety and so another section of pipe has to be inserted also. This is why the original hole cut in the canvas was made larger so that the other pipe, about one inch in diameter wider, could be placed over the smaller one so that approximately twelve inches of it is inside the caravan roof and the same amount above it. The two pipes are usually a four inch one for the longer full length and a five inch one for the safety collar. Whilst these fittings are in a temporary position, mark with chalk where the arch of the roof touches the pipe and remove both pipes from the waggon. Using this mark, which should be mid-way along the shorter of the two pipes, it will be necessary to weld a small circular collar to the top edge of this to hold it in position on the inner pipe and also to stop rainwater dripping through into the interior. At the very top of the full-length pipe add a flexible cowl to stop rain and to direct smoke from the stove. After all these sections are welded together into one, return them into the waggon via the hole, having first fixed two aluminium plates with a corresponding size hole in each, one on the inside and one on the outside screwed to the timber bows and the same width.

The Smith & Wellstood "Queenie" stove.

The front of an old Reading waggon completely stripped of paint and ready for its primer coat.

Andrew Church from Norfolk decorating one of the caravans he has made himself in time to bring one through Yorkshire en route to Appleby Fair in 1983.

Example of perfect scrollwork on a small Bow-top caravan.

Finally seal any small joints at this point with a standard filler and make sure that no fabric is actually in contact with any metal. When perfectly satisfied that everything is safe, light the fire and you will observe that the interior four inch pipe will get very hot while the larger one should keep fairly cool, thus preventing a fire to the caravan roof.

When all damaged and useless timbers have been removed, treat with woodworm fluid any exposed or infected areas. Repair all damaged parts with the same type of wood as they were originally and only use the best quality materials. When all the wood has been repaired it will need painting. Always select a good quality oil-bound paint, that is one that you clean your brushes in white spirit or turps substitute, and start with the primer coat. Do not fill any small cracks or nail holes till after this primer coat has been applied as it acts as a binder for the filler and will prevent it dropping out at a later date. When the primer coat has dried, lightly sandpaper the surface with a very fine grade paper and continue to paint with the desired coloured undercoat; red undercoat if

Shirley-Ann Jamieson working on an Open-lot caravan in the courtyard of the Costume Galleries at Castle Howard, North Yorkshire, in 1978.

the final gloss is red or maroon, greeen under green, and yellow under yellow. Sandpaper again and then add the gloss paint. At this stage you may wish to give another coat of undercoat prior to the final gloss or you may prefer to use two coats of gloss. In which event you must really sand down between coats so the shine from the first gloss is removed to act as a key for the second coat.

The outside of the caravan should be in different colours and techniques from the inside and every care should be taken to be as authentic as possible. This can be achieved by observation of those caravans still in existence, but be very careful that they have been restored correctly or you will be copying other people's errors! The interior of the caravan will have either the real polished wood found in the more expensive models or a wood grained paint effect found in the not so expensive ones.

Wood graining is a matter of covering a cheap timber with an oil-bound stained paint, adding the natural wood markings, and finally varnishing to

Burning off old paint needs great care and is not always advisable when restoring old dry vehicles.

protect it. To obtain a working knowledge of this art a simple instruction is listed below but for more advanced and detailed information any good decorating book should be of use.

After priming and filling all timber, two coats of a buff undercoat, using white undercoat with artist's oil colour or stainers in raw umber or ochre, are painted on and allowed to dry. Mix a graining medium of one-third linseed oil, one-third white spirit and just less than one-third terebine or goldsize and have to hand a tube of raw umber colour. Mix the graining medium and apply a thin coat with a brush then mix a little graining colour with some of the medium and with a small decorating brush dot it at random over the moistened surface. With a large brush spread this colour in the natural direction the grain would take, being extra careful to finish the grain when the wood does and not to trail it round corners where it would not naturally go! While still wet, flog or stipple the surface and allow to dry overnight. The following day use a brush and mix graining colour with medium on palette and paint on extra grain definition. After two or three days this will have dried and dulled off. Varnish with two or three coats to bring out all the depth and beauty of the natural thing.

Outside the caravan all the woodwork is now in its final gloss state. The underworks are usually a cream or yellow, with the top in greens, maroons or

Springs, brakes, pan bow and chamfered wheels are all shown here to good advantage.

wood-grained browns. The chamfers and carved areas will need decorating with colour and the scrolls and highlights may be attempted in gold leaf. Do not be put off by the difficulty of working in gold as the same effect can never be achieved with ordinary paint.

Gold leaf work, or gilding, is the general term used to describe the process of fixing gold to a solid surface. Since it was first used and developed over the centuries, gilding has required special skills, tools, and materials to be produced, and skill techniques to be learned. The peoples of Egypt recorded the method of manufacture in their wall painting, and evidence of their skill can still be seen on manufactured articles of many dynasties; so the Gypsies were not the first people to use this technique. The need to decorate surfaces with gold is dependent upon many factors, not just aesthetics but a combination of availability, fashion, wealth and tradition.

Gilding itself can be classified into four main divisions: oil gilding; glass gilding; water gilding; and powder gilding.

For the purpose of gypsy caravan decorations, we need only deal with oil gilding as this was the method used. All forms of gilding require careful preparation, and when oil gilding, the surface must be first prepared and primed with paint to the highest standards, whatever paint system is used. The final paint coating should be rubbed to a smooth finish without any imperfections, such as brush marks, orange peeling, or bits. The mordant can be one of a number of mediums, each having special advantages.

Japan gold sizes have gilding times between 30 minutes and 20 hours. The quicker sizes have the advantage that they are dust free sooner. When gilding outside, weather conditions may demand a quick gilding process. The faster the drying the less flow of the size. Some signwriters prefer quick drying varnishes, or paint, in place of gold size for quicker work. Old gold size or French size has gilding times from 24 hours onwards. It has the advantage of good flow, so that brush marks are eliminated, but there is a tendency for the size to heap at the lower levels of work unless care is taken to ensure even and correct film thickness on application. The gilding time, which is very critical in the 30-minute sizes, having to be judged in minutes, is much longer in the 24-hour ones, with an hour being the tolerance in certain instances.

When the size has achieved the correct degree of tack the gold is placed on the size and pressed into contact using the fleshy inside of the thumb or by using a wad of cotton wool. When gilding carved areas do the high spots first and then fill in the hollows. Take care to prevent the clean tissue paper from sticking to the size or this causes a fault in the final work. Polishing with a wad of clean cotton wood will remove ragged edges and unwanted gold. This polishing is achieved by friction rather than pressure, and when correctly done, burnishes the gold to a good lustre.

To know when the size is ready to take the gold requires a little experience but it is most simply ascertained by touching with the knuckle of one finger. The size should not wet the skin. If it does not hold to the skin it is too dry. This judgement is an essential requirement and the amount the skin can be pulled should be learned. If the size is too wet the gold will not stick, or it will smear as pressure is applied. The gold will also loose some of its lustre, and be stained.

When the gold will not cling all over the sized area it has been allowed to dry too much.

The gold itself is purchased from merchants in book form, 25 sheets 3¼″ square in either loose form or transfer with a thickness of approximately four microns at the centre. Transfer leaf is attached to a thin sheet of tissue paper and placed between two pages dusted with armenian bole. Gold quality varies but the usual one supplied is 23¼ct. which is almost as pure as you can get. If, however, you have been given some sheets that you are doubtful about you can test them to ascertain their authenticity. With a glass rod apply a few drops of strong nitric acid to the leaf. This will attack copper but have no effect on gold. Next apply (after cleaning the glass rod) a few drops of hydrochloric acid on an area near to, but not touching, the area already treated. Again this has no effect on gold but would attack the baser metals. Now draw the globules of acid together joining the two areas so that they are both under attack from the combined acids. The gold will at once dissolve. No single mineral acid will attack gold but a mixture of nitric and hydrochloric acids will, and as gold is traditionally know as the Royal metal, this mixture acid is know as 'aqua-regia,' or Royal water.

Scroll patterns can be drawn on paper first and then copied on to the area of the caravan where they are needed by chalking the reverse side and then tracing the design through. The more skilled Gypsy decorators do not use patterns but rely on their ability to draw direct the free flowing scrolls that look so well in the finished work. Whichever method you decide to use always dust down the paintwork with a fine chalk powder as this prevents the gold sticking where you don't want it to. Paint over the chalk in the pattern shape with the size and allow to go tacky prior to applying the gold leaf.

The next day when the scrolls have hardened off burnish with a wad of clean cotton wool to give an extra shine and to remove surplus gold and chalk dust.

These scrolls can now be outlined and shaded in the traditional style, which can be observed better from photographs than explained fully here. If you wish the whole area of decoration can be varnished for protection. A word of warning with regard to varnishing. Many old-time craftsmen still insist on a final varnish, even though it is now included in the gloss paint. This is a relic from the days when all paint had to be hand mixed and the gloss, or varnish, was put on last to give a good deep shine and extra protection. Nowadays the gloss is included in the final coat of paint and one sometimes gets a milky flaky effect with a varnish put onto a gloss which spoils all the earlier effort. Having said this, it is sometimes necessary to varnish over gold leaf for its protection, but a little of the reflective lustre is lost by so doing.

Lines are added round the chamfers and along the straight edges in off-white paint with special extra long lining brushes. The technique is called stringing and a good professional job can be achieved with a little practice. The long lining brushes are usually fitted into a quill and are graded to the size of the bird from where the quill originally came. Thus a fine lark liner is set into the quill from the lark and because it has a small diameter only a few hairs can be fitted into it giving a thin brush and a thin line. Duck, goose and swan produce brushes of a larger size and therefore a thicker line. Some of the modern ones

A unique caravan made and owned by Mr. Basil Smith of Guisborough, North Yorkshire, whilst living in Australia, from their local timbers. Brought to Yorkshire in a sea container in 1985 and used by him in conjunction with a brilliant children's puppet show.

have a small wooden handle to hold onto whilst working but most decorators prefer the old style quill as it is easier to hold. Always keep the liners, and all brushes for that matter, soft and clean by waxing in goose or duck fat or petroleum jelly. Place them flat in a suitable size tin with a lid and wash out well in turps substitute prior to use. By waxing in this way the shape of the liner is retained and the spring and softness of the hair is maintained for easier and better working. The paint used for lining must be thin enough to trail but not too thin so that it runs down the new paintwork. Mix on a palette and by holding the loaded liner downwards see if the paint runs off easily or stays on the brush. Experience will teach you when you have the right consistency for a good line easily applied.

Internally the caravans all have the same basic layout as described in a previous chapter and in every case the decoration tends to be more personal. The curtains normally are lace and are draped with a smart ribbon tie. Cushions and pillows may be patterned with lace edges and the table-cloths and decorative place-mats most certainly will be lace. Brass and copper all nicely polished with the Crown Derby and Aynsley china on display alongside the Waterford cut glass complete the restoration.

The preservation of the Gypsy caravan rather than the actual restoration of the same is a totally different matter.

It was never intended by the Romany people that their living units should be preserved in museums as curios for the general public. From the 1880's to the 1930's when the horse-drawn caravan was at its most popular it was a necessity for everyday living and never expected by them to have to be preserved for future generations. Times change in all walks of life and for the Gypsy people maybe quicker and more drastically. The advent of the motor car ousted the horse-drawn vehicles from the roads and their ways of making a living changed over the years from a slow idyllic pace to the faster modern way of doing things.

From the 1950's museums have shown a partial interest in the Gypsy heritage and quite a few of them around the country have the occasional example on display to the public. Generally speaking the museum services do not use a knowledgeable caravan restorer but tend to rely on their own internal staff who do not always understand the colours and patterns required. There are a few museums who do obtain skilled and experienced people to complete their restoration work and it must be said that these examples are really preserving the best of the Gypsy culture and showing the public a true picture of how things were.

The few expert restorers of this work in Great Britain normally have some vehicles on hand perhaps in a small private museum as part of their premises. Unfortunately these tend to be in South Wales, North Wales and the South of England and not in the Yorkshire area.

Examples of caravans may be seen by the public at the following museums in Yorkshire. A visit is well worthwhile.

The Ryedale Folk Museum, Hutton-le Hole, North Yorkshire.

Armley Mills, Canal Road, Armley, Leeds.

Abbey House Museum, Kirkstall, Leeds.

City of Kingston upon Hull, Transport & Archaeology Museum, Hull.

The interior of Basil Smith's caravan. Everything is designed for his comfort and use as a study for his writing when on the road.

The modern trailer – Appleby Fair.

The Castle Museum, Tower Street, York.

The Transport Museum, Aysgarth Falls, Aysgarth, North Yorkshire.

West Yorkshire Folk Museum, Shibden Hall, Shibden Park, Halifax, West Yorkshire.

For those interested in the Gypsy caravan a visit to one of the fairs is one means of seeing a working model, as many Romany people still keep a horse-drawn caravan for just such events. They are usually used at the fairs for telling fortunes, so enter inside and see what the future holds for you!

The Gypsy heritage must stay within the Gypsy people themselves and no museum, however well-intentioned, can reach the soul of the people who have travelled our country through the generations to bring a lot of common sense, colour and charm into our lives. We would not expect to intrude so let us respect and admire them when we meet and leave the mystery of the heritage with the people to whom it belongs.

CHAPTER EIGHT

THE GYPSIES' PRESENT AND FUTURE; THEIR SITES, HEALTH AND EDUCATION

In the towns, cities and even the countryside the travelling people are often hounded and moved on. The law is slightly kinder now than it used to be, but even so people cannot stop where they wish and are expected to conform and settle on a permanent site. These council-provided sites are no more than modern concentration camps and do nothing but break the travelling spirit of the people forced to live on them. What right has the non-Gypsy official to make these people conform? Just because they have a different culture why should they be made to fit in with the ways of the house-dweller? To what purpose? If this is what the traveller himself wants then by all means give him the chance to say so, but do not force him.

It is said in official quarters that it is better for the Gypsies' health. Can this really be so? Being on a site with a dozen other families in close proximity to the towns and all the germs and problems these can cause, can never be as healthy as the open road and the freedom to stop when and where desired.

Last year on returning home to the West Riding of Yorkshire a family and their baby daughter had suffered the cold, wind and wet of three weeks on the road in a horse-drawn open-lot caravan. Going back to the so-called 'normal' way of life the little girl attended her local playgroup and after a week or so the whole group of children were struck down with a dysentery bug — except the only one who had been out in the elements for three weeks!

The same family was visited by a health visitor who was horrified by their intention to return to the road once again. He claimed that their health would suffer. As he was himself full of cold and feeling rotten due to his centrally heated home and office he may have been the wrong person to advise on these matters.

The Gypsies' spirit of travel is being lost and, in fact, forced out of them. Modern generations of Gypsy children will never know a wild herb, or its uses and health-giving properties and, if the local authorities have their way, will all be processed through the state education programme and end up as bland and uninteresting as most of the non-Gypsy children.

In Yorkshire today the new compounds (for want of a better word) are being built by the district and county councils. Small concrete enclosures with council thought-out names like 'Travellers' Garth' at Malton, opened in 1985 for fourteen families. Whilst a clean and tidy site it is hidden from view behind a large earth mound at the entrance and a ten foot high fence on the other three sides. No other council or private estate in the town requires this kind of fortress round it!

Malton Gypsy site entrance.

(Top) Malton Gypsy site showing high external fencing, power cables overhead, washroom/toilet block and store.

(Bottom) Malton Gypsy site showing high external fence.

107

Clifton, York, has had a site for a few years now and Selby and other areas are busy building. Once each district has completed its site, it applies to the government for designation, which means that it has provided for its own Gypsies and others from outside the area must not come in. This system is like musical chairs with each council area trying to beat its neighbour to safeguard itself from these unwanted visitors. The reason for this is to make the traveller static and to take him from the roadside by force. The people pay a rent for their concrete flap and other facilities but the cost of building such sites cannot ever be repaid from these. It would seem more practical to build more council houses with the money and offer these to the travellers if they wished. As all sites are placed either on good agricultural land or damp ex-rubbish dumps, to build more houses would appear to be a more sensible choice.

Since the local authority amendments in 1974 many local facilities and services for all sections of the community have been changed — very few for the better as we are losing the manpower actually providing the services and gaining the manpower for those who organise them. In the case of Gypsies some areas like Bradford in the West Riding are actually employing non-Gypsy schoolteachers specially to instruct Gypsy children, not in the ways that Gypsy children have been taught for generations by their parents' example but in the ways the new authorities would like them to be taught.

The Leeds area has put a special community policeman in charge of a group of caravan dwellers. He makes regular van visits and spends all his police-time talking ,watching, and keeping his eye on the travelling population. No wonder they are jumpy at the sight of a blue uniform always on their doorsteps. This kind of pressure is never put on groups of non-Gypsies. Agreed, there are some community police in certain areas connected with the schools. They have their own 'Bobby' that the children are expected to relate to, but never has the general population had a community policeman knocking on doors and inviting himself into people's homes for no special reason.

The Church does not wish to be left out of this general desire to make the Gypsy people conform. Whereas in the past Gypsies have taken the religion of the area, or country they happen to be living in, and this may still be partly true, in Sheffield however there is a branch office of the Catholic faith that operates a mobile service for travellers with a small group of nuns and a priest, always on call and willing to travel anywhere at any time for any reason. The non-Gypsy people would be hard pressed to receive this kind of attention.

The last fifty years or so have been a very harassing time for the travelling folk. The Great War tragedy in Europe and the government and local councils' attitude to them since have drastically altered the nature and temperament of the people. Whilst many have succumbed to dwelling within four walls and have left the open road for ever, it is going to be a very different and uninteresting world without the evidence of these mysterious people on our highways and byways.

There is a belief among house-dwellers that the Gypsies belong nowhere, but it is truer to say that they have roots everywhere. They return time and time again to the same areas attracted by work opportunities and will remain as long as they are allowed and can make a living.

*The modern Buccaneer caravan made by Cobdale Trailers Ltd., Full Sutton, York,
showing a traditional horse-drawn Bow-top in the background.*

Most travellers can neither read nor write because they have had little or no formal education, but they are concerned that the future should be different for their children. Keeping Gypsy children in annexes or special classes taught by non-Gypsy teachers does not achieve anything. Travellers themselves feel that it is more sensible to educate Gypsy and non-Gypsy children together in state schools where they can come to know each other and so reduce tensions and prejudices. In the future Gypsy children will have to live alongside house-dwellers, as it is from this source that they will earn their living.

There are two factors to be considered in the present education of Gypsy children. Firstly are the assets of a natural freedom. They enjoy much love, care and attention and can play outdoors with natural materials; use their imaginative play in relation to outdoor activities as well as contact with animals and a continuous education from various members of the family geared to the eventual life they will have to lead. The other side of the educational coin is that

The interior of the Buccaneer caravan showing to full advantage the cut glass mirrors and chromework all creating the feeling of space.

Traveller child playing with antique two-wheeled cart on the Malton Gypsy site.

many children have a poor language development: No books. No pencils. No drawing. No toys inside the caravan. No cutting, pasting and sticking things indoors, because it makes a mess. No quiet private time inside the trailer because other people are always about. Little contact outside their own group, which causes prejudice and suspicion.

All things being considered the ideal situation would be to combine the best of both worlds and not necessarily come down to the lowest common denominator.

With all groups, if one wishes for change one must start with the youngsters, and since 1970 the Save the Children Fund has been offering a helping hand. This organisation works closely with the authorities concerned in the fields of health care and education at all levels including playgroups. They have a mobile clinic which takes medical and contraceptive care and advice to the families, usually at the roadside, and attends fairs like Appleby. Whilst spending most of their time with pre-school children they are one of the few organisations whose ultimate aim is to work themselves out of a job! But this will only happen when all local authorities fulfill the requirements of the 1968 Caravan Sites Act to provide sites or help families find their own sites!

Another worthwhile group helping the travelling people in Yorkshire is the Sheffield Gypsy Support Group, which runs an advice and welfare rights centre and supplies a teacher and other community workers.

It must be noted that in the past the Gypsy has wished for a life free of rules and regulations and has, because of this, sometimes deprived himself of the right to health care, education and social benefits. The present economic

111

Group of happy traveller children from the Middlesbrough area visiting the Ryedale Folk Museum, Hutton-le-Hole, in the summer of 1986.

climate, legal restraints on the siting of trailers and licensing of vehicles, and the need to fill in complicated forms, have brought them in closer touch with those around them. Gypsies still have no inclination to change their basic culture but are gradually coming to acknowledge the value of education and health care. Whilst Sheffield seem to be filling a very worthwhile need a similar group in York has just had to close due to lack of funding.

After the Second World War the authorities tried to organise the Gypsies' lives for them. The fear at the time was that the bureaucrats would form a group of inspectorates of camping grounds. This fear passed but the inspectorates were brought in under the new administration set up in 1974. Many things have changed, maybe for the worse, in this organisation of people's lives. The original boundaries were altered, causing confusion to the people as well as the postman. Children might have to attend different schools because the one they would have gone to was now in a new area. Rates were paid by house-dwellers to a reorganised larger authority. The staffing levels of these new large bureaucratic machines continues to increase and the service they are supposed to supply decreases.

The local authority expects travellers to conform. It dictates that they should move to, and live on, little concrete islands. Whilst they may enjoy the benefit of running water (tap — not spring) and a shower, they do not always have the room to continue their chosen trades. It may seem all well and good to herd people together against their will but factors like diseases have never been taken into consideration. In normal life the traveller would move around his chosen area in a small family unit, from one job to another during the year. He would be out in the fresh air and almost immune from all group ailments. Today on a site with maybe fifteen other families if one suffers they all do!

In matters of hygiene nature has always looked after its own. The chain of evolution has provided ways of clearing away its own waste. Washing is provided by clean fresh streams and clothes are also laundered in this way. The non-Gypsy is not used to all this natural cleanliness and depends on washing machines, chemical washing powders, soaps and other devices to keep himself clean.

The planning of organised sites presents the problem of where to put them. The moment one is suggested no person living nearby wants it to be in his area. Only waste land away from everyone is ever offered to the travelling people — old tip sites, motorway junctions or old railway sidings. Anywhere out of sight and out of mind.

The Gypsy does not really wish to draw attention to himself but to continue about his everyday business in the quiet unassuming way that he has always done. Sometimes, by the time the villagers had realised he was camped nearby he had moved on! This speaks volumes for the low profile usually kept. To be placed on a special camp site draws attention to the Gypsy and attracts both local troublemakers and the police to the site at the first sign of problems, whether or not caused by the site occupants.

Travellers should never be organised. Time to them never matters as jobs get done when they need to. If visitors call for a chat and a cup of tea, so be it; the jobs will still be there when they have finished. There is no nine to five attitude with the travelling people though they may work harder and longer making a living than their non-Gypsy counterpart. Planning and the Gypsies do not go together. Leave them to wander the countryside (what is left of it) to give us pleasure with their free ways, and allow us to envy them their way of life.

Sadly all of us, not only the Gypsies, are being regimented to conform. This starts at school, no, at birth as each child's details are fed into a computer and at regular intervals during his life he receives papers and documents to sign. He is expected to conform. Never forget that in the two World Wars the British Gypsy contributed as much as the house-dweller in the hope of retaining his freedom. Unfortunately local and other authorities do not recognise their contribution.